DRAW
Me NEARER

A HIGHLY FAVOURED LIFE DEVOTIONAL

31 days with Him

VOLUME 1

ISBN:
978-1-967189-19-9 (paperback)
978-1-967189-20-5 (hardback)

Table of Contents

Our Roadmap 9
By Marissa Patton

Winner not a Whiner 15
By Deborah South

Transformed 21
By Hannah Suttle

Thinking About Home 25
By Grace Shiflett

Beautifully Broken 29
By Katie Ledbetter

Sorrow is Better 33
By Lydia L. Riley

An Unexpected End 37
By Kelly Byrley

Down but not Destroyed 43
By Victoria Kiker

Do Good 47
By Alicia Moss

Rest in His Shadow 51
By Kay Reese

Stay - Not Quitting During the Dry Season 55
By Cristy Tadlock

Our Refuge in Times of Calamity 61
By Lisa Petersen

Thinking Done God's Way 67
By Jenny Young

Are You Holding a Grudge? 73
By Judy Rolfe

What is God Preparing for You? 77
By Debra Birner

Handfuls of Purpose 83
    By Coretta Gomes

Confident and Content with Conflict 89
    By Wanda Davidson

Slipping Away: Encouragement to Hold Fast 95
    By Misty Wells

Finding God's Will 101
    By Hannah Kasprzyk

Trust the Driver 107
    By Marsha Leto

Purple Paint: A Lesson in Obedience 113
    By Sarah Russell

Our Spiritual Garden - Growing in Christ 119
    By Cherith Shiflett

Be a Jochebed 125
    By Beverley Wells

Hey, Zeruiah, the 'Maintenance Required' Light is On! . . 131
    By Kim Thompson

Renew My Spirit 137
    By Rikki Beth Poindexter

Rest in the Lord 143
    By Susan Hutchens

Lessons Learned in a Trial 149
    By Lois Van Zee

The Strength of the Lord 155
    By Anja Meyer

Spiritual Step Count 161
    By Rainy Lehman

Don't Follow Your Heart 165
    By Elizabeth Garrett

A Look at Joseph 171
    By Renee Patton

Dedication

This devotional is dedicated to the godly ladies God
has placed in our lives who gave us a good example of drawing
closer to God. They not only gave us a good example
but also encouragement as we walked along life's way.

Introduction

"Draw me nearer..." This beautiful phrase composed as a song makes us shed a tear during a Sunday morning service. Maybe it hung as an art piece on the wall of a dear saint of God endeavoring to keep her heart right each day. Some of us may even have the verse James 4:8 as our life verse. But drawing nearer to God comes with obstacles as well as victories.

It looks different for each woman in each season of life. One lady draws closer to Him during a season of full surrender to His will. Another takes a step closer to Christ as she lets go of the anger and bitterness she has harbored for so long. Some lady draws closer to God by removing the sin that drags their heart from the Savior. A weeping woman draws closer to Him by calling out for strength during the darkest trial of her life while a joyful lady draws closer to Him in her season of current "perfectness."

No matter which one of these women you are, it should be your desire to draw closer to Christ every day. As another song says, "nothing between my soul and the Savior." Our prayer is that this collection of devotionals will motivate you to clean your heart, clear your mind of Satan's devices, and come closer to the One Who loves you so. Our prayer should be, "Draw me nearer, Lord."

Our Roadmap

By Marissa Patton

Thy word is a lamp unto my feet, and a light unto my path.

Psalm 119:105

I am directionally challenged. Anyone else second that? Kudos to those of you who can give directions better than my GPS. When we were on deputation to go to the mission field, we took turns driving. I always drive with a GPS. I do not care if I am in an area I am familiar with. The GPS is my "security blanket."

One trip, we decided to spend Valentine's Day weekend in Waco, TX. I was driving. My husband was navigating me from the passenger seat with the GPS on his phone. He told me to follow 35E South to Waco. I told him that there was no way I was going to remember that. He said, "Well it should be easy to remember because it is Exit 467B." That was when my brain sort of shut down. As we got closer, the freeway got busier. The interstate signs overhead became more overwhelming. There were blue badge-shaped signs and big rectangle green signs. White and black boxed speed limit signs giving various numbers – not to mention, there were exit signs with fast food labels and gas station stops.

God's Word is not meant to be an afterthought in life.

My husband told me that we were turning pretty soon. Now at this point, I was really confused! Finally, I asked him if he would let me follow the GPS for a while to make sure that we actually made it to Waco on time. Once I saw the bright screen showing me each turn to take, I was confident again. We laughed at my obvious struggle to drive from memory of his directions. We made it to our destination safely with minimal mental trauma on my part.

As I thought of this story, I was convicted and reminded of something important. God's Word is our GPS for our day-to-day travels. We are on the road of life. During our Christian journey, there are distractions that are constantly popping up. A friend's birthday party requires a run to Dollar General for a card and gift. An unexpected fever has us reaching for the phone to ask our spouse to grab some children's Tylenol at the pharmacy. A work meeting during the week causes us to miss a night of revival. Accidentally waking up late for school makes us rush out the door forgetting to spend time in God's Word. You can insert your own distraction here.

So many times, we get so caught up in the "road signs" of our busy life that we forget to consult the GPS to make sure we are actually still on track. God's Word is not meant to be an afterthought in life. It is the most valuable Resource we have for making sure we reach the end of our Christian journey safely. Proverbs 3:6 "In all thy ways acknowledge him, and he shall direct thy paths." There is no substitute for following God's Word in your life.

Here are some helpful tips to making sure His Word is your sole navigator.

1. Schedule time. We schedule time for family and doctor's appointments. We take time to scroll through social media. Why not make time to have devotions? Schedule a time in your busy day to consistently be with God.

2. Choose the best part of your day. If you are a morning person, read your Bible in the morning before the day gets started. If you are a night owl, set a time before bed to get in some quiet time with the Lord. If you function better after a cup of coffee or a hot shower, put your Bible reading time after that.

3. Be accountable to someone. Find someone to share your devotional thoughts with throughout your week. Have a friend that you text every few days with something God gave to you in your reading. Sit down with your spouse often and tell him what you have been studying.

4. Write it down. Keep a bullet journal to get your thoughts organized and look back at those thoughts when times get tough. Underline and circle key words in your reading that spoke to you. These little tools are a great encouragement when the devil throws up unexpected road signs.

Do not be like me and try to navigate "alone." Use the roadmap God has given you. My prayer is that one day, I will reach my destination hearing, "Well done, thou good and faithful servant."

DRAW
Me NEARER
Today in ...

"*I am Thine, O Lord, I have heard Thy voice,*
And it told Thy love to me;
But I long to rise in the arms of faith,
And be closer drawn to Thee."

Winner not a Whiner

By Deborah South

In every thing give thanks: for this is the will of God in Christ Jesus concerning you.

I Thessalonian 5:18

I love skits! I like watching them. I like participating in them. I like writing them! I am not necessarily good at it, but I do enjoy trying. Over the years, I have had the fun of helping in Vacation Bible School and Youth Camp writing skits and participating in them.

One skit at Vacation Bible School that I particularly enjoyed (and my husband hated) was the "Wendy and Wanda Whiner" skit. If anyone has seen this, you know how annoying it can be. My friend and I would come down the aisle whining loudly about literally everything. "The room was too hot. There are too many people. The singing was too loud. The preacher always preached too long. Someone took my seat!" You get the picture. By the time the skit was over, the whole crowd was tired of us and our whining. The VBS leader would then explain that the reason we were whining so much is because we had forgotten to be thankful. He would quote verses on thankfulness to try to help us to be grateful.

How many times are we like Wendy and Wanda Whiner? How many times do people want to avoid us because of our whining attitude?

15

Often we forget how good God has been to us and how blessed we are. Did you eat today? Did you have clothes to wear? Were you able to use your legs to get out of bed and your arms to tie your shoes? Were you able to wash your hands and take a shower or bath? Did your washing machine and dryer work today? What about your dishwasher? Did you drive your car or bicycle to where you needed to go? I could go on and on, but I think you understand what I am writing about.

We can become so ungrateful that we can become discouraged and depressed at life because things are not turning out the way we think they should. Circumstances have not gone our way. If you make the mistake of dwelling on this life, yourself, and your circumstances, you can become a miserable, whining wreck. You will not want to be around you and neither will anyone else.

It is easy to get discouraged when we get our eyes off of the Lord.

Depression can sneak in, and the devil can tell us how badly life has gone for us. If we are not careful, we will begin to listen to our old, deceitful flesh. And truly, we will not be the first to have this battle. John the Baptist, David, and Elijah also encountered depression. But the Lord can help us even at our lowest points.

Here are a few thoughts that will hopefully help you become a Winner, not a Whiner!

1. Count your blessings! The songwriter said, "Count your blessings, name them one by one...." I heard a preacher once say, "Count your blessings, name them ton by ton!" If we have nothing else in this life except salvation by the grace of God, we can truly say we are blessed! Do not forget to thank God for

all He has done for you and the people He has put in your life. Encourage yourself in the Lord.

2. Think of someone else! Do not just think of yourself, especially when you begin to get discouraged or depressed. When I was young, I never remembered my mother being one for many words. When she was asked for advice, she always had a great amount of wisdom in her answer. I attribute her wisdom to the time she spent with the Lord. I remember ladies asking my mom what they could do to help them with their discouragement. They had situations that truly could have caused a great amount of depression. My mom would say, "Go find someone who is hurting or in need and help them! Stop thinking about yourself for a moment. You cannot focus on yourself and your hurts when you are focusing on someone else and their hurts." Such true words. I would watch the ladies who took her advice come back with smiles on their faces because they had been able to put a smile on someone else's face. When discouraged, look for someone else who is in need of a meal, a phone call, a cup of coffee, a kind note, an understanding conversation, whatever is needed, and be that one that makes the difference!

3. Sing! Ephesians 5:19, "Speaking to yourselves in psalms and hymns and spiritual songs, singing and making melody in your heart to the Lord." There are so many good songs that can lift you up and help you change your way of thinking when you are "speaking to yourself!"

4. Celebrate good days! Sometimes we feel that we are too discouraged to ever get back up. Everyone has bad days. Some have bad weeks; some have bad years. However, with the help of the Lord, you can have those blessed days; You should celebrate them! Call others to rejoice with you. If they are true friends, they will be thankful for what God is doing in your life.

Do not neglect your Bible and your prayer time! You will need the power of the Lord to help you meet the stress and strain of daily life that comes. No matter what, make time for the Lord. I have a friend who wrote a song recently about how this "one thing is needful" to spend time with the Lord. Life will get in the way if you do not have a plan to spend time with the Lord. I understand there are days it can be hard. I recently kept my two grandsons for two days while my daughter and son-in-law were out of town. When they returned, I gratefully gave her the two boys (whom I love dearly) and laughingly said, "I will never fuss at you for not reading your Bible until midnight, or if you do not clean your house for days, or even if you do not have time to shower. I am worn out!" Yes, life happens. Sometimes you will not be able to do all you want to do but do not neglect the Bible (even if it is just a few verses!).

This is by no means an exhaustive study on winning over discouragement, but these are a few simple things that can help you be a winner and not a whiner!

DRAW Me NEARER
Today in...

"I am Thine, O Lord. I have heard Thy voice,
And it told Thy love to me;
But I long to rise in the arms of faith,
And be closer drawn to Thee."

Transformed

By Hannah Suttle

And be not conformed to this world: but be ye transformed by the renewing of your mind,
that ye may prove what is that good, and acceptable, and perfect, will of God.

Romans 12:2

This is a verse we have all heard before. How we should flee from sin and strive to be more like Christ has been preached consistently from the pulpits. It is easy, however, when the emotion of the service is over, to quickly become lackadaisical and forget about taking action upon those convictions. We do the obvious things: we are at church for every service and are faithful to our tithes and offerings. We have good dress standards, and have our kids enrolled in the Christian school. We make sure we read our Bibles regularly and give a little gift basket to the missionaries when they come through. We have lived up to the standard of "being an exceptional Christian," being different, and not conforming to the world.

I was recently convicted that we have made the mistake of thinking that "not conforming" and "transforming" are the same thing. During a lecture in one of my college classes, our teacher, Pastor Robert Simpson, made this statement, "Just because it isn't sin, doesn't make it acceptable." As Christians, the goal of our life should be to please the

Lord in everything that we do. When we walk with God, there will be things that we cannot do and feel as if we are pleasing God at the same time.

For instance, staying up late on Saturday and watching a movie is not a sin, but you are not as rested in body or as prepared in spirit for the service as you could have been if you had gone to bed earlier. Eating three pieces of cake is not a sin, but it is not taking as good of care of your temple as you could have if you only ate one slice. We are so good at following the rules and doing the right thing, but I am afraid that more often than not, it is out of habit instead of desire. We are being careful not to conform to the world, but we are not taking any extra steps to be transformed to the mind of Christ.

I do not want to just be "not conformed." I want my life to be lived for the purpose of pleasing my Saviour. I want to be transformed to be like Christ. I want His love to shine through me, whether it be my attitude or my actions. I want my mind to be renewed to be constantly thinking of things that I can do to glorify God. I want to prove His will for my life, and that will is serving Him with my whole heart. I want to encourage you to take this challenge too!

Look for little things in your everyday life that you can do to glorify God just a little bit more than you did the day before.

DRAW *Me* NEARER

Today in...

"*I am Thine, O Lord, I have heard Thy voice,*
And it told Thy love to me;
But I long to rise in the arms of faith,
And be closer drawn to Thee."

Thinking About Home

By Grace Shiflett

But if we hope for that we see not, then do we with patience wait for it.

Romans 8:25

Home. Just the word makes me have all the wonderful feelings. I think of peace, rest, anticipation, loved ones, safety, and the list goes on and on. These thoughts warm my heart when I think of home.

But throughout the course of our lives, "home" as we know it can change. Maybe from the loss of a loved one. Maybe it is from family division or the need to relocate. Not all changes are because of bad circumstances. I am simply saying that our earthly home can change. Sometimes it's just from the need to start afresh.

The older I get, the more I find myself longing for home. Not the place where I was raised or the various places my family has lived. I'm talking about my final home – heaven, the place Jesus has gone to prepare. Heaven is where our faith will become sight! There we will see face-to-face the One who died for us. Heaven is the sweet home of the soul. There will be no more disappointments, no tears, or sin. There we will be reunited with loved ones and saints who have gone on before us. What a glad reunion day when we get to worship our Saviour for all eternity!

To be honest, we can never imagine how magnificent the place is that God has prepared for us, His children. I am so thankful for the promise that He is coming again someday to take us "home!" According to the Apostle Paul, we can comfort one another with the reminder of our future home. "Then we which are alive and remain shall be caught up together with them in the clouds, to meet the Lord in the air: and so shall we ever be with the Lord. Wherefore comfort one another with these words, " I Thessalonians 4:17, 18.

We should be thinking about and talking about heaven constantly. It is our comfort and hope for born-again Christians. "Looking for that blessed hope, and the glorious appearing of the great God and our Saviour Jesus Christ," Titus 2:13.

Are you looking for His appearing? If you are, are you looking with excitement or dread? "But if we hope for that we see not, then do we with patience wait for it." Romans 8:25

Let me encourage you to meditate on your future, permanent home – heaven. Let heaven be a common topic in your conversation. Tell your friends and family all about that home that is prepared for those who love the Lord. In these desperate times in our world, we need to be reminded of the hope of heaven more than ever before! We can be filled with excitement because this unstable world is not our home. Let us look toward heaven with anticipation knowing that the Lord is coming soon to take us to heaven – our perfect home!

More Reading:
John 14:1-6; I Thessalonians 4:16-18;
I Corinthians 2:9;II Timothy 4:8; Hebrews 11:16

DRAW Me NEARER

Today in...

"*I am Thine, O Lord, I have heard Thy voice,*
And it told Thy love to me;
But I long to rise in the arms of faith,
And be closer drawn to Thee."

Beautifully Broken

By Katie Ledbetter

*And the vessel that he made of clay was marred in the hand of the potter:
so he made it again another vessel, as seemed good to the potter to make it.*

Jeremiah 18:4

Learn in life not to give people the freedom to fix you. The more people know your struggles, the more mission-minded some seem to set to work making sure you become their project to restore. When you don't "fix" easily, the expectations go up. You feel like you're failing them, and you begin to perceive that you're a burden to their success. Bearing one another's burdens is about getting under the load not trying to remove it. The Lord is not breaking you so my confidence can be bolstered in fixing you. He is breaking you for Himself, for His glory.

Jeremiah 18:4, "And the vessel that he made of clay was marred in the hand of the potter: so he made it again another vessel, as seemed good to the potter to make it."

Pray for true encouragers in your broken times. Encouragement comes only from those willing to let you be broken and allow you the luxury of not meeting unattainable expectations. Encouragement comes from a heart that whispers prayers for you in the night watches. Encouragement comes from those willing to love your brokenness.

Those who see the workmanship God is doing in you for His honor and glory. Encouragement comes not from pity but from praise for all the Lord is doing in your life before you ever see the outcome.

May we all become like Paul and say: Philippians 4:11-12, "Not that I speak in respect of want: for I have learned, in whatsoever state I am, therewith to be content. I know both how to be abased, and I know how to abound: everywhere and in all things I am instructed both to be full and to be hungry, both to abound and to suffer need."

When we are broken and suffering or watching others who are and we desperately want to help fix what we see broken, may we remind ourselves to be content in knowing that the Lord is the Potter. We can rest in His hands and allow others to do the same without our interference. Sometimes we are marred in His hands on purpose simply so He can make us again. Learn to be beautifully broken.

The broken are used to help the hurting like nothing else can (Job 2:7-8). Your brokenness may never be whole again, but it may be the very thing the Lord uses to give relief to someone hurting in ways you could only imagine. What I've learned from brokenness is that it is never about me. It is all about the Lord being able to use me either as broken or as another vessel entirely. I want to be a useful vessel. He may want me to be a broken potsherd. When I'm determined to serve His purpose, I will stop caring about what I look like in the end. He may want to fashion me into a lovely vessel or just something used to give someone else just a bit of relief as they scrape their mess onto my life. I can learn how to truly encourage them.

May we be willing, no matter how He sees fit to use us, to rest in the Potter's hand, beautifully broken until He sees fit to make us again.

DRAW Me NEARER

Today in...

"*I am Thine, O Lord, I have heard Thy voice,*
And it told Thy love to me;
But I long to rise in the arms of faith,
And be closer drawn to Thee."

Sorrow is Better

By Lydia L. Riley

Sorrow is better than laughter:
for by the sadness of the countenance the heart is made better.

Ecclesiastes 7:3

This life is full of sorrow - some so intense and breathtaking that our whole world seems to crumble at our feet. This truth in God's Word might be a shock – but the Bible states that sorrow is better than laughter ... why? Because by sadness, the heart is made better.

A good question to ask ourselves is, "Is my sorrow making me bitter or making me better?"

According to the very next verse (Ecclesiastes 7:4), wise people know the value of mourning. When suffering from a bitter loss, allowing the healing steps of grief can make us stronger, wiser, and better. How can sorrow make my heart better?

First of all, remember that God uses godly sorrow to bring repentance and salvation into our lives; God is often working behind the scenes to bring about the most beautiful act of redemption in the midst of true sorrow over our sin (II Corinthians 7:10).

As a Christian, how can the sorrows of this life make me a better person?

Sorrows make us more compassionate. Sorrows make us more caring. Sorrows make us more Christlike. Sorrows make us more compelling.

II Corinthians 1:4-5 states "Who comforteth us in all our tribulation, that we may be able to comfort them which are in any trouble, by the comfort wherewith we ourselves are comforted of God. For as the sufferings of Christ abound in us, so our consolation also aboundeth by Christ." Show the compassion and care of Christ to someone else when they are hurting.

Jesus Himself was a "man of sorrows and acquainted with grief...." When we go through suffering, we come to know our Saviour in a more intimate way and can, in some small way, relate to His great sacrifice and the suffering He endured for us. We become more like Christ.

I Peter 3:18 shows the truth that Christ's suffering was so that He could bring us to God! Is my suffering making my life more compelling to others? Can we allow God to also use our sorrow and suffering to bring others to Himself?

Remember that sorrow does not last forever, joy does come in the morning. Psalm 30:5 "... weeping may endure for a night, but joy cometh in the morning."

I Peter 5:10 "But the God of all grace, who hath called us unto his eternal glory by Christ Jesus, after that ye have suffered a while, make you perfect, stablish, strengthen, settle you."

Our suffering is for "a while" -- it won't last forever -- God has plans for your life - to perfect you, stablish you, strengthen you, settle you.

Don't be destroyed by your sorrow -- allow the Lord to truly make you better and not bitter. Only by His Grace can this be accomplished. For Better or for Worse? The choice is mine; the choice is yours. Choose to believe that HE is faithful

DRAW
Me NEARER
Today in...

"*I am Thine, O Lord, I have heard Thy voice,
And it told Thy love to me;
But I long to rise in the arms of faith,
And be closer drawn to Thee.*"

An Unexpected End

By Kelly Byrley

For I know the thoughts that I think toward you, saith the Lord, thoughts of peace, and not of evil, to give you an expected end.

Jeremiah 29:11

Have you ever read those books that allow you to choose your own adventure or choose your own ending? I can remember reading them when I was a little girl. They were so much fun! If you are not familiar with these types of books, let me explain the basic idea. You would come to a point in the book where it would give you two options of which pages to turn to in order to continue the story. Some books would give little clues about what could happen if you turned to one page or the other and some books would not. You would make your choice, and then you would come to another point in the book where you would be given another set of page numbers.

This would continue a few more times depending on the book until you reached the end. I always loved to go back and re-read the same book and choose different options every time. I would get a different story and a different ending every time. Depending on the book, there could be dozens of different stories and outcomes. Sometimes the pages I chose led me to fun and exciting adventures and sometimes they led to bad or disappointing ones. If I ended up with a choice that led to disappointment,

37

Living right is always worth it.

I would just re-read the book and choose another page number when I got to the place that had led me down a not-so-great path.

This is great for fictional reading, but not for real-life living. In real life, there are consequences for taking the wrong path.

There are no do-overs. Our choices in real life matter. They affect us and those around us. They affect those who are watching and following us. They affect the lost. They affect our ministries and our church. They affect eternity.

When the Lord is writing our story, there are many times when we will come to the pages of our life that have options. But unlike those books, the Lord makes it crystal clear which options have good outcomes and which do not. There is no guessing on which one we should choose and what will happen if we choose the wrong one.

His Word very clearly lays this out in Deuteronomy 28. Verses 1-2 show God's blessings for those who turn to the right pages. It says, "And it shall come to pass, if thou shalt hearken diligently unto the voice of the Lord thy God, to observe and to do all his commandments which I command thee this day, that the Lord thy God will set thee on high above all nations of the earth: And all these blessings shall come on thee, and overtake thee, if thou shalt hearken unto the voice of the Lord thy God."

In contrast, verse 15 is a warning to those who are about to turn to the wrong page. It says, "But it shall come to pass, if thou wilt not hearken unto the voice of the Lord thy God, to observe to do all his commandments and his statutes which I command thee this day; that all these curses shall come upon thee, and overtake thee...." Verse 45 is even more of a warning. It mentions that the cursings will not just overtake us, but they will pursue us and destroy us.

We will be overtaken either way, but whether it is being overtaken by blessings or cursings is solely determined by which pages we turn to in our life's book.

There are countless times the Lord tells us in the Bible what will happen when we do right and what will happen when we do wrong. He has an expected end for us, but that does not mean we cannot change that into something that is not His expected end for us. Our choices determine our end. Every time we come to a page in our life where we have to make a choice, we are choosing our end. These pages can be daily pages, weekly pages, monthly pages, and so on, but each and every one matters.

Each and every page has the potential to change our story and our ending. If you have been turning to the right pages so far in your life's story, I implore you to continue. The Lord's expected end is always the best ending possible. An expected end means there is an expected path. His path for our lives is always the absolute best with the greatest amount of favor, blessings, and protection.

Living right is always worth it. Please look around at the people you know who had a great life story, but then turned to the wrong page one day. Their lives are probably a mess or on their way there. I cannot tell you how many people I know that are facing a far worse ending than they ever dreamed. If that is you and you have been turning to the wrong pages, do not lose hope! It is never too late to make the right choice today.

You may still have scars, pain, and baggage from all the wrong choices you have made, but the Lord will forgive you, and He will bless your obedience moving forward.

DRAW *Me* NEARER

Today in...

"*I am Thine, O Lord, I have heard Thy voice,
And it told Thy love to me;
But I long to rise in the arms of faith,
And be closer drawn to Thee.*"

Down but not Destroyed

By Victoria Kiker

We are troubled on every side, yet not distressed; we are perplexed, but not in despair;
Persecuted, but not forsaken; cast down, but not destroyed; Always bearing about in the body
the dying of the Lord Jesus, that the life also of Jesus might be made manifest in our body.

II Corinthians 4:8-10

A while back, my family went through a difficult time in our lives. One day while in prayer, I began asking God why He would allow such a difficult trial in my life. With a heavy heart, I flipped open my Bible with no real direction in mind and came across these verses in II Corinthians.

Like Paul, although in very different circumstances, I too was feeling everything he felt. I was troubled seemingly "on every side." There was no good news coming my way, and I didn't know if there would be any light at the end of this dark tunnel. I was "perplexed," even feeling a little persecuted. You know, the "Why me?" attitude. My heart and mind were "cast down."

The shadow of overcoming depression began to loom as I became more and more overwhelmed with the unknown. Ever been there?

I knew I'd have to combat my feelings by encouraging myself in the Lord (I Samuel 30:6). Yes, I was troubled, but I didn't have to be distressed (to suffer from anxiety, sorrow, and pain). Jesus had already "bore my grief and carried my sorrow" (Isaiah 53:4). I was, and am still at times, perplexed. But I'm not in despair. He knows my need,

43

and my situation. Nothing has taken Him by surprise! I may have felt persecuted, but I have never been forsaken. My gracious, loving Father "will never leave me, nor forsake me" (Hebrews 13:5). I have been cast down in spirit, but this has not destroyed me. In fact, it's caused me to build a deeper, more intimate relationship with my Lord.

Then the Lord in His great mercy opened up this Scripture in a way I'd never seen it before. Verse 10 gave me the real reason why I believe God allowed this circumstance in my life: "that the life also of Christ might be made manifest in our body." This trial had not come to just teach me a lesson so that I could pass the proverbial test. It came so that Christ Himself would be made manifest in me — in my body.

The word "manifest" means "to be clear or obvious to the eye or mind." I began to question, is it "clear and obvious" that God is in me as I walk through this trial? When people see my family and me treading these dark waters, do they see the grace of God and the joy of Christ, or do they see us troubled, perplexed, and cast down?

Above all else, I desire for Christ's life to be seen in me. He is worthy to be honored and glorified no matter the situation I find myself in — good or bad.

How about you, friend? Are you going through a troubling time? Maybe a time when you have no idea how things will turn out? I encourage you to allow Christ to be seen above all else. No matter the outcome, the Lord will be faithful to you. Trust Him! Pray and ask Him for strength. And when you don't know what to pray (I've been there many times), know that He understands and will intercede on your behalf.

I'll leave you with a quote by C.H. Spurgeon. He said, "God is too wise to be mistaken. God is too good to be unkind. And, when you can't trace His hand, you can ALWAYS trust His heart."

44

DRAW Me NEARER
Today in...

"I am Thine, O Lord, I have heard Thy voice,
And it told Thy love to me;
But I long to rise in the arms of faith,
And be closer drawn to Thee."

Do Good

By Alicia Moss

As we have therefore opportunity, let us do good unto all men,
especially unto them who are of the household of faith.

Galatians 6:10

Have you ever thought, I wish I could serve the Lord better? Or, I wish I could sing better, have a greater prayer life, or be closer to the Lord? Sometimes, we want to rate our service to the Lord. "I made a 100 percent today because I..." or "Man, I'm a failure today because..."

Many times as Christians we see the great giants of the faith, and we want to serve the Lord in the same capacity. How did the great giants of the faith become great? What is one small thing we can do to serve God greater? Do good!

Galatians 6:10, "As we have therefore opportunity, let us do good unto all men, especially unto them who are of the household of faith." The word "good" in this verse means "benefit" or "well." How is our service to the Lord benefiting all men? How is our politeness? How are our manners in secular locations? Are we doing good to the waitress who just can't seem to get the drink order right? The end of the verse states, "especially unto them who are of the household of faith." How are we benefiting our Christian brothers and sisters in Christ?

Are we looking for opportunities to serve our Christian family? Is there a widow who needs a ride to church? Is there someone who needs a home-cooked meal or a Doordash meal? Are we looking for opportunities to do good?

I am guilty of having a one-track mind of "xyz" must be done today and forgetting to look for opportunities of doing good to all men. Should I be good to the leaders in my church? Sure, but what about the teenager who is looking for answers. How can I find an opportunity to do good? What about the widower who could use a smile of encouragement?

Acts 10:38, "How God anointed Jesus of Nazareth with the Holy Ghost and with power: who went about doing good, and healing all that were oppressed of the devil; for God was with him."

GOOD = philanthropic = seeking to promote the welfare of others.

Paul instructed us to do good in Galatians, but even Christ modeled doing good in Acts. As Peter preached about Jesus in Acts 10, he listed Christ doing good by being anointed and healing the oppressed. Wow, who would have thought doing good would equal healing the oppressed? We can't heal the oppressed, but we can do GOOD!

I challenge us to be aware of the opportunities to do good to all men. Ask God to allow you to see how you can do good to all men. Can the time God has given be shared? Can the money God has blessed you with be given?

What talent do you have that can benefit someone?:
- a poem
- a crocheted pot holder
- a pot of soup
- a prayer
- a loaf of sourdough bread
- an encouraging note

Look for the opportunities to do good!

48

DRAW Me NEARER

Today in ...

"I am Thine, O Lord, I have heard Thy voice,
And it told Thy love to me;
But I long to rise in the arms of faith,
And be closer drawn to Thee."

Rest in His Shadow

By Kay Reese

He that dwelleth in the secret place of the most High
shall abide under the shadow of the Almighty.

Psalm 91:1

The Lord brought this verse to my memory and how He used it in my life. Psalm 91 portrays so much that takes place under His shadowing. Song of Solomon 2:3 reminds us of sitting down under His shadow with great delight.

Long ago when my children were younger, we moved into a triplex apartment that had a giant oak tree hovering over the part we lived in. We had gone there to set up a new life for ourselves. Unfortunately, we had separated from their dad. Our lives were left unsure of what would happen! Finances were low, and I had no job at that time. My husband wasn't able to give us much money, and sometimes I was not sure that he would if he did have the money.

All of us stayed with my pastor's family and saved enough to get the apartment. So, we moved in with very few belongings and lots of uncertainties, but God hovered over our lives like that mighty tree! We were under His protection and watchful care! He sent my wonderful church family and friends our way who were used to helping us so much. We did not have a car, but someone was always there to pick us up when the church doors were open. Time and time again, He moved, and under His shadow, we rested.

He supplied every need as He has never failed to do! Deuteronomy 31:6 says, "...he will not fail thee, nor forsake thee." There are countless stories of my physical needs being met, as well as my emotional and spiritual needs. He helped me with all that was going on. I eventually got work and odd jobs to pay my bills.

In Psalm 91, His Word says that He is my refuge and that His love is set upon me, along with Him being with us in trouble. What great delight this brings! The Lord desires us to always stay close to Him in prayer and in reading His Word. He wants to overshadow our lives!

He is Almighty and provides rest, reassurance, guidance, and quietness.

I would like to say I have always rested in His shadow. However, many times I have wandered out. Abiding near our Lord is what He deserves! He is so good to us! Lamentations 4:20 talks of others seeing us "living there under His shadow."

This will bring glory to His name. I often go by that place where I used to live and many memories of the Lord's love and mercy flood back. I look at that old tree still standing, and I say to myself, I am thankful for the shadow of the Almighty!

Since those days, I have seen His work over and over in my life. I am amazed at it all! May we all find our rest in His shadow, no matter what this life here brings our way.

Stay - Not Quitting During the Dry Season

By Cristy Tadlock

By faith Noah, being warned of God of things not seen as yet, moved with fear, prepared an ark to the saving of his house; by the which he condemned the world, and became heir of the righteousness which is by faith."

Hebrews 11:7

Once upon a time (Just kidding! I'm not writing a fairytale), I was at an odd place in one of my personal roles where things were fine. Just fine. Not great. I've been serving and following God long enough to know things can be great. I know God only wants great things for me and my family. I was playing the piano, and I had chosen the song "I Have Decided to Follow Jesus." Out of the sincerity of my heart, I was playing it as a prayer to God that I would follow Him anywhere, wherever His will was. And it was like I heard God ask my heart, "What if I just want you to stay? What if I want things to stay exactly the same? What if things are just 'okay' for a while?"

I flippantly responded, in my heart, of course, that's easy. I'll just continue. But the longer I played, the more convicted I became.

55

Am I willing to stay? Am I willing to stay in the hard place without seeking a way out?

Am I enduring the stay or thriving in the stay? I believe God wants the best for His children. He will give the best to those that live for Him. So in my flesh, I only want to dwell in those times of complete goodness. But let's be real. Sometimes, getting to the best is a process. Sometimes, it's just about staying with God. That's when I realized, this could be God's will for a looooong time. Only God knows! This could be exactly what God wants for me, even if I don't think it's the best.

Can I stay? Can I be content in trusting in Him regardless of the "spot" of life I'm in? Consider this. We recently started a new year. So, 89.75% of us just finished reading Genesis according to our Bible reading plans right? Well, think of Noah. We know God used Noah greatly. We know Noah trusted God immensely. Noah actively obeyed God. I mean, y'all, he built an ark ... by hand! It doesn't get more active service than that.

But Noah also served during the staying spots. Noah trusted God during the staying spots. Noah wasn't begging for change during the staying spots. In Genesis 8, the rain has stopped (v. 2), the earth isn't completely covered in water (v. 3), and the ark is resting (v. 4). Noah waits forty days and opens a window to send out a raven and a dove. He had to be hoping, "Please, let it be time to get off this boat."

But the dove returned. So Noah "stayed yet other seven days" (vs 10). Then he sent forth another dove; that dove returned in the evening with a leaf in its mouth. Imagine the excitement. Surely, it's time to leave. But do you know what Noah did? He stayed on the ark seven more days (vs 12).

Noah knew how to stay. Even when he knew that this wasn't God's final plan. He didn't rush ahead to get to the good part or become discontent and pitch a fit because he was done with that spot in life. No. Noah simply stayed.

Can I stay during the difficult spots? Do I just endure the staying spots, or can I enjoy the staying spots? I can if I want to! How? Just by trusting. Making up in my mind that God knows what He's doing, and I'm here for the long haul. He loves me too much to do me wrong. I need to rest and stay until He says to move. So I challenge you to stay...

1. Stay during seasons.

Marriages, families, and churches go through seasons just like the weather. Is your marriage in a summer season of dryness? Stay during the dryness. As a wife, continue to obey your commission given by God and just hang on for the fresh breath of fall. Is your church in a winter season of coldness? If you have a sound doctrinal church, I encourage you to stay. I've been an active church member since the day I was saved over twenty-five years ago. Guess what? It's not always easy! Services aren't always amazing. But guess what's coming? The new life and fruit of spring. Stay!

2. Stay when it's not fun.

Marriage is not always fun. Motherhood is not always fun. Being an active church member is not always fun. But be mature and stay in the place and role that God has called you to. Don't ditch family events and responsibilities or church services because "it's not fun right now." Stay!

3. Stay during transitions.

Every role that you occupy in life has transitions. As a young lady, you transition to a wife. As a wife, maybe you transition to motherhood. As a mother, you transition through the empty nest period. As a church member, you go through pastoral changes. As a woman, you go through physical transitions. And maybe, all of the above. It's hard...every. single. bit of it. But what should you do? Stay!

God's best is on the way. I believe it. I cling to it. He wants only good for me. So I will rest in God. Rely on God. Trust in God. He will give me the strength to stay.

DRAW Me NEARER

Today in...

"I am Thine, O Lord, I have heard Thy voice,
And it told Thy love to me;
But I long to rise in the arms of faith,
And be closer drawn to Thee."

Our Refuge in Times of Calamity

By Lisa Petersen

Be merciful unto me, O God, be merciful unto me: for my soul trusteth in thee: yea, in the shadow of thy wings will I make my refuge, until these calamities be overpast.

Psalm 57:1

What is a refuge? The dictionary describes it as "a protection or shelter, as from danger or hardship."

God is our refuge when hardships and challenges come into our lives. He wants us to run to Him as our Protector. He wants to comfort us and carry us through our troubles. Finding God's truth and running to Him for refuge in the storms of life is the only way to survive those storms.

After two decades of unmolested peace as a missionary in Africa, I was stunned when a thief broke into our home and stole some things. I told my pastor that I truly felt my faith was shaken, and he looked at me and said, "No it hasn't been." He quoted to me two verses that I will not forget. One was I Corinthians 10:13, "There hath no temptation taken you but such as is common to man: but God is faithful, who will not suffer you to be tempted above that ye are able; but will with the temptation also make a way to escape, that ye may be able to bear it." The other verse was Romans 8:28, "And we know that all things work

61

together for good to them that love God, to them who are the called according to his purpose."

Little did we know that, soon after, we would face one of the most difficult trials of our lives as someone would seek to use lies to steal from us and to harass us. In this dark time, I had to run to Jesus for my comfort and refuge.

When facing trials, it is easy to become angry, hurt, bitter, hopeless, or unforgiving. But God can deliver us from those things if we find our refuge in Him.

Isaiah 32:2 sums up the idea that God is our refuge. "And a man shall be as an hiding place from the wind, and a covert from the tempest; as rivers of water in a dry place, as the shadow of a great rock in a weary land." We know that "a man" in the verse is, ultimately, the Lord Jesus. He is all of these things for us and more. We need to let the Lord be our hiding place, our shelter of protection, our provision, and our pavilion for an escape from times of heartache.

David knew that God was his refuge. He had people that were after him and, at times, he had to run for his life. We know from the Psalms and what we read there, what a refuge God was for him. With Isaiah 32:2 as our guide, let's look at some of these verses.

1. A refuge is a place to hide.

"And a man shall be as an hiding place from the wind," Isaiah 32:2(a). Psalm 91:2, "I will say of the Lord, He is my refuge and my fortress: my God; in him will I trust." God wants us to have 100% confidence in Him, even when things look hopeless. He smiles on His children when they have complete trust in Him. Psalm 142:4, "I looked on my right hand, and beheld, but there was no man that would know me: refuge failed me; no man cared for my soul."

Here, the Psalmist says he could not find refuge anywhere. No man cared for him. Can you imagine that lonely feeling he was going through? He truly felt no one cared for him. I know that I have felt very lonely at times, in different seasons of my life, but I knew that many people loved me and cared for me during those times.]

I hate the devil. He will make it seem that God doesn't love us or care about us when we go through difficult things, but that is a lie. God does truly love His children. Even though David didn't feel that any man could help him, he knew God would. In the next verse, he says, "I cried unto thee, O LORD: I said, Thou art my refuge...."

2. A refuge is a protection from the storms of life.

And a man shall be as ..."a covert from the tempest;" Isaiah 32:2(b). Psalm 46:1, "God is our refuge and strength, a very present help in trouble."

In trouble, He is always nearby. In times of calamities, we need a refuge for our soul until they are past. Psalm 62:7, "In God is my salvation and my glory: the rock of my strength, and my refuge, is in God." If we can trust Him for salvation, we can trust Him that His strength and grace will help us through the storms of life. Nothing we go through is beyond His ability to protect us and deliver us. We know, as His children, that God is bigger than the storms and trials of life and that we will never go unprotected. Whatever situation we are in at this moment, we can be assured that God is with us! We just have to start believing this!

3. A refuge is a provision of refreshment.

And a man shall be ... "as rivers of water in a dry place," Isaiah 32:2(c). Psalm 142:5, "I cried unto thee, O Lord : I said, Thou art my refuge and my portion in the land of the living."

David knew that God was all he needed. He was his portion. He knew God would refresh him in a dry place. Jesus said in John 7:37-38, "... If any man thirst, let him come unto me, and drink. He that believeth on me, as the scripture hath said, out of his belly shall flow rivers of living water." When we believe on Jesus, He becomes our refuge of provision and refreshment.

4. A refuge is a pavilion for escape.

And a man shall be ... "as the shadow of a great rock in a weary land." Isaiah 32:2(d)

A pavilion is a shelter that provides shade from the harsh elements of nature. Psalm 91:1 "He that dwelleth in the secret place of the most High shall abide under the shadow of the Almighty." The Lord is a shade for us in a weary land. He will shelter us from the heat of the battles we face. Psalm 9:9, "The Lord also will be a refuge for the oppressed, a refuge in times of trouble." David knew God was a refuge for those oppressed by the harsh elements of this world, a safe place to go to in trouble.

Loving God, loving His Word, and applying it to our lives, especially during trials, is how we see God as our refuge. When we look at problems and trials in light of God's Word, instead of Satan's lies, then we will truly see the love of God, the comfort He can bring, the miracles He will perform, and the refuge that He truly is for us.

DRAW *Me* NEARER

Today in ...

"*I am Thine, O Lord, I have heard Thy voice,*
And it told Thy love to me;
But I long to rise in the arms of faith,
And be closer drawn to Thee."

Thinking Done God's Way

By Jenny Young

Finally, brethren, whatsoever things are true, whatsoever things are honest, whatsoever things are just, whatsoever things are pure, whatsoever things are lovely, whatsoever things are of good report; if there be any virtue, and if there be any praise, think on these things.

Philippians 4:8

How many thoughts does one think in a day? It is stated that the average person thinks about 6,000 thoughts a day if they sleep for eight hours. When I consider it, that statistic is staggering. How many thoughts do I think in one day? Do I really want to know the answer to that?

I do not know about you, but I do a lot of thinking during my day. I find my thoughts can determine my attitude and how I treat others. My thoughts are very powerful and controlling. How can such a small thing affect so much of my life? It's because my life is based on what and how I think. Everything that I do involves thinking.

My thinking can get me into more trouble than I care to admit. I tend to overthink and make assumptions. My mind can easily conjure up something that is nowhere close to being true. Controlling my thought life is one of my weaknesses. I often think the opposite of how God would have me think.

I just recently completed a study on Philippians 4:8. Why? So that I can better my thinking and see how God wants me to think. I want to share some of my studies with you.

1. True Thoughts.

Truth is "a true state of facts or things." According to this word, I should think about that which is built on truth and not lies. Why? Because if I think about the lies, it means I am listening to my flesh; I am allowing my flesh to control and take over my thoughts. If my thinking is built on that which I know is true, it is God that I am listening to. He will never make me think about something false. Truthful thinking means that I am allowing God to control my thoughts.

2. Honest Thoughts.

Honest is "the thought of being upright, just, fair in dealing with others; free from trickiness and fraud." My thinking should be fair toward others. Being fair means not jumping to conclusions or assuming what others are thinking. I do not know the motive or the thoughts of others. I should never assume that I do. But, it is something that I am guilty of doing. I assume things based on a look, a simple text, or a passing conversation. I should be fair in the thoughts of others and take them for who they are and what they have said.

3. Just Thoughts.

The word just means "that which is free from sin or sinful affections or desires, or thinking that is innocent (free from guilt)." This could refer to even thinking about past mistakes and failures I have made along the way. When I stop and ponder my past, I'm overcome with guilt. God does not desire for me to live and think that way. God has forgiven me. I must remember that forgiveness when my mind tries to dwell on my past.

4. Pure Thoughts.

The word pure means "properly clean, innocent, modest, and perfect." For my thoughts to stay pure and clean, they must stay focused on God and the truth. God does not want my mind to be clouded with the filth of this world. Having pure thoughts means I must guard my thought life and consider my thoughts. I must ask God to keep them pure, and then, I must guard my own mind.

5. Lovely Thoughts.

The word lovely carries with it the thought of being friendly towards others. If I am friendly towards someone, that means I am at peace with them. My thoughts should be the same way – centered on peace. If I can keep my thoughts peaceful, they can stay lovely no matter what happens during the day. Lovely thoughts are thoughts that must be adjusted daily. Why? Because they can leave just as fast as they come if I am not careful.

6. Thoughts of Good Report.

God also wants me to think on things that are of a good report. The words good report are thoughts that are "reputable or well-spoken." The word reputable means "not mean or disgraceful." When my thinking is negative, my thoughts are of little worth or value to me. Why? Because negative thinking produces negative actions. Anything in life that has a negative sign in front of it has no value or worth to it. My thoughts should be positive. That is when they are valuable and of worth. God desires for my thoughts to be productive. I cannot be used by God if my thoughts are negative.

7. Thoughts of Virtue.

Virtue is "strength or valor." It is thinking outside the box and constantly learning – not learning about the world, but learning about God and His Word. It is having a deeper thinking of the characteristics of God. The more I know about God and God's Word, the more strength I have to face my enemies. My mind is weak and frail when I have not kept my thoughts on the things of God. True strength comes from God, and I can only have that strength by thinking of Him.

8. Thoughts of Praise.

The word praise also means "laudable." My thinking should be praiseworthy and healthy. Negative thinking is not healthy thinking. Negative thinking can bring about depression and low self-esteem. However, when I am praising God for how good He is to me, I have a healthy mind. Positive thinking produces a life of impact because I see my life as being used by God.

When I praise God in my thinking, I can only praise Him for the good and positive, for He is nothing but good! Not once does Philippians 4:8 tell me to think on things that are wrong or unfavorable. Every word listed is positive. Why? Because God knows that negative thinking only leads to a poor outcome. God knows how much my thoughts control me.

God wants me to praise and have thoughts of value. II Corinthians 10:5 says, "Casting down imaginations..." For me to carry out Philippians 4:8, I must cast down or bring into captivity all my imaginations and thoughts unto the obedience of Christ. What is the obedience of Christ? It is thinking the way that God wants me to think. It is thinking that lines up with God's Word.

The Lord has given me every tool I need to have a proper thought life, it is just up to me to use the tools He has given me. Unfortunately, I do not choose to think the way God wants me to think every single day. But I do not want that to keep me from striving to daily think the way God wants me to think. Think positive. Think God's way!

DRAW
Me NEARER
Today in...

"I am Thine, O Lord. I have heard Thy voice,
And it told Thy love to me;
But I long to rise in the arms of faith,
And be closer drawn to Thee."

Are You Holding a Grudge?

By Judy Rolfe

And when ye stand praying, forgive, if ye have ought against any: that your Father also which is in heaven may forgive you your trespasses. But if ye do not forgive, neither will your Father which is in heaven forgive your trespasses.

Mark 11:25-26

A pastor recently said, "A short memory and a forgiving heart are best." The consequences of unforgiveness are very real and detrimental in so many ways.

Each time we begin to pray, God will remind us if there is someone in our life that we refuse to forgive.

Our prayers will be hindered by this unforgiving spirit.

So often we wait for the other person to ask forgiveness first. Meanwhile, our prayers go unanswered, and we develop a critical spirit. The person who forgives little will also love little. Luke 7:47, "Wherefore I say unto thee, Her sins, which are many, are forgiven; for she loved much: but to whom little is forgiven, the same loveth little."

People are going to offend us. The question is – How do we respond? Do we allow our minds to mull over and over what they said or did? This only makes us an unhappy, miserable Christian.

God's Word actually teaches us to be the first to go and reconcile our fellowship with that individual.

This requires humility on our part. Our pride wants to avoid that person and criticize them before others.

I have been deeply hurt by others, as I am sure most everyone else has at some point in their life. How we respond is what really matters. As you read this, if the name of someone comes to your mind that you have not forgiven, ask the Lord to give you the courage and humility needed to go to that person and reconcile things.

The burden you have been carrying will suddenly be lifted, and you will know a peace that passes all understanding. Unforgiveness causes stress and anxiety. Forgiveness is the very best medicine.

Let those grudges go. You will never regret it.

DRAW
Me NEARER
Today in...

"I am Thine, O Lord. I have heard Thy voice,
And it told Thy love to me;
But I long to rise in the arms of faith,
And be closer drawn to Thee."

What is God Preparing for You?

By Debra Birner

... Go, do all that is in thine heart; for the Lord is with thee.

II Samuel 7:3

Have you ever wanted to do something great for God?

For some of us, we may want to help another person, maybe feed them when they are hungry. Perhaps that's something we want to do for God. Our Pastor has grown our church in many ways and preached all over the world – he has done something great for God. On Saturdays, some of us go out and knock on doors of people we don't even know, to tell them how they can put their trust in Jesus Christ and be saved – we are trying to do something great for God.

Well, King David wanted to do something great for God. In II Samuel 7:1-3, we read:

"And it came to pass, when the king sat in his house, and the LORD had given him rest round about from all his enemies; That the king said unto Nathan the prophet, See now, I dwell in an house of cedar, but the ark of God dwelleth within curtains. And Nathan said to the king, Go, do all that is in thine heart; for the LORD is with thee."

The great King David had built for himself a house of cedar. King David loved the Lord. And he wanted to do something great for God. He looked at what he had and thought, "Wow, I want to build a house for God." He was excited and went to God's man and said, "Hey, I want to build a house for God."

But then, we read the next verses: II Samuel 7:4-7 "And it came to pass that night, that the word of the LORD came unto Nathan, saying, Go and tell my servant David, Thus saith the LORD, Shalt thou build me an house for me to dwell in? Whereas I have not dwelt in any house since the time that I brought up the children of Israel out of Egypt, even to this day, but have walked in a tent and in a tabernacle. In all the places wherein I have walked with all the children of Israel spake I a word with any of the tribes of Israel, whom I commanded to feed my people Israel, saying, Why build ye not me an house of cedar?"

Have you ever wanted to do something great for God, just to find out that's not what God wanted from you? Disappointing?

Sometimes, we go through life our own way, and we know we are not going in the direction God has for us. But sometimes, we feel like God throws us a curve. We think we are doing right, but then we find out God has different plans.

78

Read the rest of this discussion that King David is having with Nathan and with God in II Samuel 7:8 - 11.

God is saying to David, let's talk for a minute about doing great things ... let's talk about the great things I have done for you. I took you when you were nothing, just a shepherd boy. I made you into a great king. You talk of building a house – I make a place for my people. "I will plant them, that they may dwell in a place of their own." I have given my people rest.

God is saying, "I am the great provider. I can make you into something. I have made you a great king. I have provided for the people that you lead. You have rest from your enemies that you may enjoy what I have given you."

But there's more ... with God, there is always more.

What is God's response to David wanting to build him a house? He says no, you won't build me a house ...

Let's finish verse 11, where we stopped short before the end: II Samuel 7:11 (end part), "Also the LORD telleth thee that he will make thee an house."

Wait a minute ... did God just say, no, you won't build me a house. I will build you a house?

David is saying to God, I want to do something great for you ... and God says, No, David – I want to do something great for you!

Oh, yes, that's exactly what he said, because he also says it in I Chronicles 17:10 (last part), "Furthermore I tell thee that the LORD will build thee an house."

Psalm 37:4 says: Delight thyself also in the LORD; and he shall give thee the desires of thine heart.

When we delight in God, he wants to give us the desire of our heart – but I'll tell you something else – He gives me even more than I desire. Because I don't always desire what's best for me. He gives me what I need.

Why is God going to build a house for David? Because David is going to need one!

There is some discussion about David's son building a house for God, and then we read in II Samuel 7:25, And now, O LORD God, the word that thou hast spoken concerning thy servant, and concerning his house, establish it for ever, and do as thou hast said.

Additionally, in I Chronicles 17:25, David is speaking, "For thou, O my God, hast told thy servant that thou wilt build him an house: therefore thy servant hath found in his heart to pray before thee."

Let's look at John 14:2-3: In my Father's house are many mansions: if it were not so, I would have told you. I go to prepare a place for you. And if I go and prepare a place for you, I will come again, and receive you unto myself; that where I am, there ye may be also.

What is God preparing for you?

DRAW Me NEARER

Today in...

"I am Thine, O Lord. I have heard Thy voice,
And it told Thy love to me;
But I long to rise in the arms of faith,
And be closer drawn to Thee."

Handfuls of Purpose

By Coretta Gomes

Thou hast given him his heart's desire, and hast not withholden the request of his lips. Selah.

Psalm 21:2

And let fall also some of the handfuls of purpose for her, and leave them, that she may glean them, and rebuke her not.

Ruth 2:16

I love the book of Ruth! There is so much to glean from it! Recently while reading through it, the phrase "handfuls of purpose" caught my attention. Those "handfuls of purpose," or those desires of the heart, come from our heavenly Father! As I reflect back over this past year, I can name several times where I prayed for a need and the Lord answered not only my need but gave me far more than even the desires of my heart.

Even more special is when you see God giving your children the desires of their hearts. My daughter shared with me how God had given her a desire of heart even though she didn't even ask for it and had told no one about it. I simply told her, "That is just how our heavenly Father is!" Just as we parents want to give our children a special treat from time to time, our heavenly Father gives us those "handfuls of purpose."

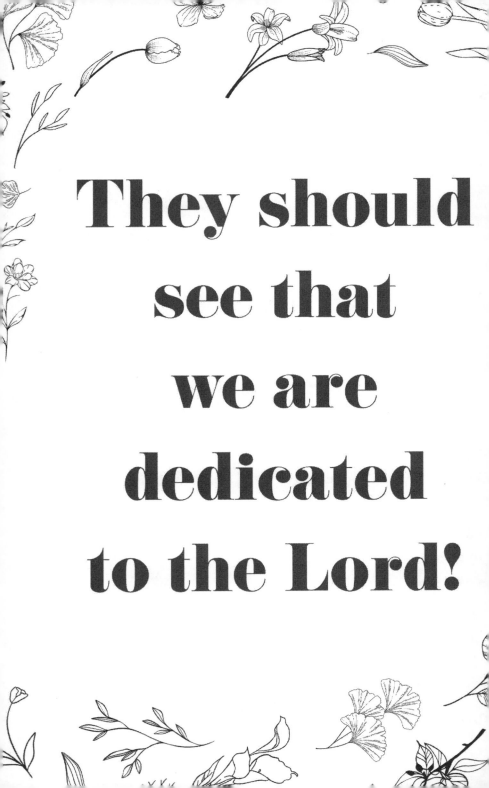

They should see that we are dedicated to the Lord!

But why would the God of Heaven give us those "handfuls of purpose" and show favor? There were a few things that I noticed in Ruth's life that can be applied to our Christian walk.

So how did a lowly Moabitess receive "handfuls of purpose" and earn such favor?

First, we see how Ruth left everything and everyone behind to follow Naomi and her God, "... thy people shall be my people, and thy God my God" (Ruth 1:16). The Bible doesn't go into detail, but I can imagine that her friends and family told her she had lost her mind to follow Naomi into an unknown land and serve Naomi's God, how she would not be able to see them ever again, and that she was abandoning her family. We all have them, those family members and friends who think we are crazy to want to live right or believe that we are being "overboard" or overprotective with our children.

However, none of this deterred Ruth. She must have seen something in Naomi's life that gave her the desire to have a relationship with Naomi's people and her God. As Christians, we leave those things and relationships behind that are not pleasing to God. Our desire should be to please our heavenly Father, not our friends, family, and this world.

Secondly, we see that Ruth had a servant's heart, "... Let me now go to the field..." (Ruth 2:2). She was willing to labor with her hands. Working in the field is hard work! For sure she was hot and sweaty, most likely had blisters on her hands, sore feet and legs, and an aching back. We do not read about her grumbling and complaining. None of these things deterred her from doing what she knew had to be done. She was determined to bring home enough food for Naomi and herself.

We should not be afraid of hard work or above doing the "dirty" jobs.

We should have a servant's heart no matter what task is set before us and do our best with a joyful spirit. I think of Ruth as being a sweet and loving person – one who did her job with the right kind of spirit and not begrudgingly.

Lastly, we see Ruth's devotion. Her reputation as a dedicated daughter-in-law had preceded her. "... It hath fully been shewed me, all that thou hast done unto thy mother in law ...." (Ruth 2:11). Boaz had already heard throughout the town of her devotion to Naomi. He saw in Ruth one who was willing to dedicate her time to take care of her mother-in-law. We should be dedicated to taking care of our families' needs both physically and spiritually.

Most importantly, they should see that we are dedicated to the Lord! Nothing speaks louder than our actions!

The book of Ruth is a reminder of God's favor toward those who serve Him with a genuine heart. Psalm 37:4 says, "Delight thyself also in the LORD: and he shall give thee the desires of thine heart." By following Ruth's example in our lives, our heavenly Father treats us with those "handfuls of purpose" when we delight in Him. I do not deserve God's many blessings, but when I follow, serve, and devote myself to Him, our heavenly Father will show His favor by giving those "handfuls of purpose"-- those desires of the heart!

DRAW Me NEARER

Today in...

"I am Thine, O Lord. I have heard Thy voice,
And it told Thy love to me;
But I long to rise in the arms of faith,
And be closer drawn to Thee."

Confident and Content with Conflict

By Wanda Davidson

Because he hath set his love upon me, therefore will I deliver him: I will set him on high, because he hath known my name. He shall call upon me, and I will answer him: I will be with him in trouble; I will deliver him, and honour him.

Psalm 91:14-15

Title down; ready to write! My brain, however, says, "That title is arrogant!" Noah Webster defines arrogant as "having the disposition to make exorbitant claims of rank; giving one's self an undue degree of importance."

But, I am not writing about my abilities; rather, what can be accomplished when I allow God to live through me! I am nothing but a sinner saved by grace. Yet, the Creator of heaven and earth Who is all-knowing wants me to represent Him and accomplish His will on earth. I must be confident in His sufficiency and content to serve Him if I accomplish His will.

In II Timothy 1:9a, Paul tells Timothy, "Who hath saved us, and called us with an holy calling, not according to our works, but according to his own purpose ...." The Scripture makes it clear, all who are saved have a holy calling on their life.

89

God has entrusted us with the Word of life – the only hope for a lost world.

In Genesis 45:8 Joseph told his brothers who had sold him into slavery that it was not them that sent him to Egypt, but God. Joseph had a divine detour with a purpose! Genesis 45:5b, " ... for God did send me before you to preserve life." Joseph's submission to God's purpose in His life benefited the Egyptians and the people of Israel, as well as influenced the course of history! Now, God has sent us to make sure that the lost around us hear the gospel. How do we fulfill the purpose God has for our lives?

First of all, to fulfill His purpose, we must stay close to God ourselves. Because we have experienced His great love, we should love Him. If we truly love Him, we will accept His will as our will. If we trust Him and stay close to Him, we will not question Him. A close relationship with God gives us the confidence to serve Him. He knows what is best for us. He is in control. He can be trusted. He may not give answers, but He always gives grace.

Psalm 91:14-15 is God speaking to us. "Because he hath set his love upon me, therefore will I deliver him. I will set him on high, because he hath known my name. He shall call upon me, and I will answer him; I will be with him in trouble; I will deliver him, and honor him."

Real biblical faith is us trusting God to do whatever He wants to do through us.

Secondly, we must stay focused. Pastor Randy Barton said, "I am on a quest for Christ!" A quest is an endeavor to reach a goal by any means necessary. No room for half-hearted Christians! We must keep our eyes on the Saviour. The disciples, while looking at the storm around them, forgot that they had the God-man, who fed five thousand and who healed the sick, in the boat with them. Jesus asked them,

"Why are ye fearful, O ye of little faith?" Fear is the opposite of faith. Fear is a snare. Adversity and the fear it brings have derailed many Christians. Joseph faced a life of adversity. Sold into slavery, lied on, cast into prison, forgotten about – but he remained focused and faithful. He became a great leader in his time of adversity.

I recently heard about a sister-in-Christ who has cancer that God "had given her great grace." Others could see God's grace in her life because grace was greater than the cancer to her. She is also being a leader in her conflict. Our God knows all about the condition of the world and the adversity that we will face. What may look impossible to us does not strain God! Jesus tells us in Luke 18:27, "... The things which are impossible with men are possible with God." Submit yourself and trust Him to do a work through you. When we make God our main focus, others will notice, and God will be glorified.

Thirdly, stay in the fight. Yes, it is a fight, and the devil has many tactics to distract us from what God wants us to do. Not only should we stay close to God, but we must distance ourselves from sin and worldliness. I Peter 1:16 says, "....Be ye holy, for I am holy." II Timothy 2:21 tells us, "If a man therefore purge himself from these, he shall be a vessel unto honour, sanctified, and meet for the master's use, and prepared unto every good work." Both of these verses are commands to keep ourselves in a usable condition.

Joseph is a good example of keeping himself in Genesis 39:12 so that God could use him, "And she caught him by his garment saying, lie with me: and he left his garment in her hand and fled, and got him out." Joseph encountered a distraction that could have destroyed his testimony. As has been said many times, "He lost his coat, but not his character!" Oh, how we need to protect our testimony in this lost world!

David, a man after God's own heart, failed to protect his testimony and mourned the consequences for the rest of his life. David experienced Isaiah 59:2, "But your iniquities have separated between you and your God, and your sins have hid his face from you, that he will not hear." Several years ago, a survey was done on a large number of random people asking what they knew about the Bible character David. The first answer was always the story of David and Goliath, but the second answer was always his adultery with Bathsheba and the murder of Uriah. What do we want people to remember about us? Does the world see us laying aside holiness and embracing more and more of the world's philosophies?

Has the devil slipped the world into our hearts and homes through the internet, cell phones, or other distractions that he comes up with?

Finally, stay on your knees. Pray for wisdom. James 1:5," If any of you lack wisdom, let him ask of God ... and it shall be given him." Add Psalm 139:23-24 to your daily prayer life, "Search me, O God, and know my heart: try me, and know my thoughts: And see if there be any wicked way in me, and lead me in the way everlasting." Pray as Jesus did in Matthew 26:39b, "... Not as I will, but as thou wilt." Remember the promise of James 5:16b as you pray "... The effectual fervent prayer of a righteous man availeth much." There will be a harvest in our lives. Our choices will decide if it is a harvest of praise to God or a harvest of shame for ourselves.

God help us to yield our will to His and serve confidently because we know that we are on the winning side.

DRAW
Me NEARER
Today in...

"I am Thine, O Lord, I have heard Thy voice,
And it told Thy love to me;
But I long to rise in the arms of faith,
And be closer drawn to Thee."

Slipping Away:
Encouragement to Hold Fast

By Misty Wells

Therefore we ought to give the more earnest heed to the things which we have heard, lest at any time we should let them slip

Hebrews 2:1

"Hold on tight!" I say as I walk my precious little ones across the busy parking lot. "There are cars pulling in and out, and Mommy would be so upset if something should happen to you." I squeeze their little hands tightly as they try to keep up with my pace. Occasionally, they begin to slip as the distractions of their surroundings steal their attention. "Hold on tight. We are almost there," I say. Their safety is most important to me, and the walk is quite pleasant, so long as they listen and heed my instruction. Sometimes we discuss the dangers around us. Other times, we talk about how pretty the flowers are. I enjoy our time together more than they will ever know. You see, it's not my desire to drag them to our destination. I would much rather them walk with me willingly, hand in hand.

The Bible says in Hebrews 2:1, "Therefore we ought to give the more earnest heed to the things which we have heard, lest at any time

95

we should let them slip." In this verse, the word slip means "to slip away from." In a world of countless distractions, are you slipping away? I want to encourage you to hold fast!

Hold fast to your profession of faith. Hebrews 10:23 says, "Let us hold fast the profession of our faith without wavering; (for he is faithful that promised;)." Do you remember the day that you came to faith in Christ? Oh, the peace of sins forgiven! It was the first time you realized that He longed to walk with you. He reached down with those hands of mercy and picked you up, dusted you off, and He placed you into the family of God. You will never have to walk alone again. Praise the Lord! Don't let the joy of your salvation slip away!

Hold fast to Instruction (the Word of God). The Bible says in Proverbs 4:13, "Take fast hold of instruction; let her not go: keep her; for she is thy life." Proverbs 4:4 says, "He taught me also, and said unto me, Let thine heart retain my words: keep my commandments and live." It's still right to obey the truth. According to Joshua 1:8, in doing so you are making your way prosperous! Listen to instruction and apply it to your life. His Word is like water to a thirsty soul. Reading the Word of God every day must be a priority. You are hindering your walk with God if you let this slip. "Thy testimonies are wonderful; therefore doth my soul keep them." Psalm 119:129.

Hold fast to tradition. Paul says in II Thessalonians 2:15, "Therefore, brethren, stand fast, and hold the traditions which ye have been taught, whether by word, or our epistle." The word tradition here simply means "what is handed on." We have been given a priceless treasure by those before us. Lessons and experiences of God's faithfulness are

96

passed down from generation to generation. Habits and disciplines formed from sound doctrine that have paved the way for others. I'm so thankful for a godly heritage. I learned how to study the Bible and pray because the importance of such things was passed down to me. I learned the necessity of faithfulness first through faithfulness in the lives of others. "Remember them which have the rule over you, who have spoken unto you the word of God: whose faith follow, considering the end of their conversation" Hebrews 13:7. These traditions are not what saved you and me, but they encourage and exhort us in the faith. We must not let them go.

Hold fast despite your surroundings. Revelation 2:13 says, "I know thy works, and where thou dwellest, even where Satan's seat is: and thou holdest fast my name, and hast not denied my faith ...." This is a message to the church of Pergamos. God is acknowledging the fact that He knows where they are. He knows how bad it is. However, the chapter goes on to tell us that the Lord has "somewhat against them" because they have allowed false doctrine into the church. Yes, they were holding fast to His name and had not denied the faith, but they were also accepting false teaching. As a mother, I wouldn't allow a stranger to hold the hand of my child as we walked along, so why should we expect God to? I refuse to hold both the hand of our Lord and the hand of false doctrine. Don't get distracted by your surroundings. Keep the pace. Hold on to righteousness and truth no matter how acceptable sin is in some of the churches of our day. We are getting too comfortable in this world. This is not our home. He has a better place prepared for His children. "But now they desire a better country, that is, an heavenly: wherefore God is not ashamed to be called their God: for he hath prepared for them a city" Hebrews 11:16.

Lastly, hold fast unto the end. "For we are made partakers of Christ, if we hold the beginning of our confidence stedfast unto the end;'' Hebrews 3:14. I encourage you to finish the way you started. Many are compromising on convictions they have held to for years. Just because society deems it acceptable doesn't mean God does. "Be ye steadfast, unmovable, always abounding in the work of the Lord ..." I Corinthians 15:58. Sinners are looking for consistency and stability in those who call themselves Christians. Please don't disappoint them. It's okay to stay the same if the same is what thus saith the Lord.

Hold fast to your profession of faith. Hold fast to instruction. Hold fast to tradition. Hold fast despite your surroundings. Hold fast unto the end. Like I say to my little ones as we walk hand in hand, "Hold on tight," for we are almost home.

Hand in Hand with Jesus
by Johnson Oatman, Jr

Once from my poor sin-sick soul
Christ did every burden roll,
Now I walk redeemed and whole.
Hand in hand with Jesus.

In my night of dark despair,
Jesus heard and answered prayer,
Now I'm walking free as air,
Hand in hand with Jesus.

When the stars are backward rolled,
And His Home I shall behold,
I will walk those streets of gold,
Hand in hand with Jesus.

Hand in hand we walk each day,
Hand in hand along the way,
Walking thus I cannot stray,
Hand in hand with Jesus.

From the straight and narrow way,
Praise the Lord, I cannot stray,
For I'm walking everyday,
Hand in hand with Jesus.

98

DRAW *Me* NEARER

Today in ...

"*I am Thine, O Lord, I have heard Thy voice,*
And it told Thy love to me;
But I long to rise in the arms of faith,
And be closer drawn to Thee."

Finding God's Will

By Hannah Kasprzyk

Redeeming the time, because the days are evil. Wherefore be ye not unwise, but understanding what the will of the Lord is.

Ephesians 5:16-17

Many years ago Corrie ten Boom very wisely stated, "Every experience God gives us, every person He puts in our lives is the perfect preparation for the future that only He can see." I absolutely love this quote! As a young person, I would read it over and over as I wondered and dreamed of what my life would be like. The future can be both scary and exciting all at the same time! It amazes me how God uses everything and everyone in my life to shape me more into the person He wants me to be.

As a teenager and young adult, I remember asking questions like: How do you find God's will for your life? How will I know what God wants me to do, who to marry, and where to go? These are big questions a lot of young people wonder about. Maybe you have even asked this as well. Being in the center of God's will is something every Christian should constantly strive for no matter what stage of life you find yourself in.

The good news is that God is not hiding His will from you. He wants you to know His plan for your life more than you do. So, how do you find God's will, you ask? Here are some things I have learned in my life.

First of all, you'll find out God's future will for your life as you do God's daily will for you today.

Yes, it really is that simple! Proverbs 3:6 tells us "In all thy ways acknowledge him, and he shall direct thy paths." There are many things that we know we ought to do as a Christian to live right and serve God. (See Matthew 6:33, Mark 12:30-31, Ephesians 6:1-2, and I Corinthians 10:31.) God wants us to do what we know is right to do today and be found faithful. When He sees He can trust us to do the little things, He will entrust us with the next step. It is a growing process. Every experience is molding and shaping us more like Christ – you can't rush the process. As you do God's daily will for your life, He will begin to reveal His future will to you step by step.

As you seek God's will, don't overlook the importance of developing yourself into a person God can use.

God has gifted each person with a unique set of talents and abilities that He wants to use. Too many teenagers may falsely think they can spend their teen years however they want and then get serious about God and find His will when they graduate from high school. God wants to start preparing you as soon as you will let Him. Don't make the mistake of waiting until you are "older" to begin learning life skills and developing talents. The Bible says in Ephesians 5:16-17, "Redeeming the time, because the days are evil. Wherefore be ye not unwise, but understanding what the will of the Lord is." Let me encourage you to discover what you are good at and develop your talents so that God can use you. Prepare now so that when God opens a door, you are ready to walk through it.

Another very important step towards finding God's will is complete surrender.

Is there anything you are holding back from God that He cannot have or you won't let Him use? If so, that is going to hinder you in your search for His will. Lay your all on the altar and give God full control over your life. Remember if God calls you to it, He will see you through it. God will not ask you to do something that He will not enable you through His strength to do. You never know what amazing things God will do with a person who is completely surrendered to Him.

As a teenager, I often wondered what God would have me to do with my life. I had the privilege to attend many youth rallies, youth conferences, and teen camps. Early on, I surrendered to do whatever God wanted me to do. I had no clue what that could be, but I was willing to do whatever. I began to get busy doing God's daily will and getting involved in the ministries of my church – nursery, Wednesday night kids program, bus route, singing in the choir. I also had a big desire to learn to play the piano. As I developed that talent, it became clear

I wanted to go to Bible college and study music after high school. It was through attending Bible college that I not only developed my skills as a pianist but also began to learn how to teach (and met my future husband). At first, my thoughts were to simply be a church pianist and teach piano lessons. Before my time in college was over, God had directed my path to be an elementary school teacher in Maryland. Today, I not only teach piano and music classes but also teach in the Christian school and serve in my local church in a variety of children's ministries and the music ministry. Looking back now after having been happily married for six years and working in the same ministry for the last nine years, I am amazed at how God has led me each step of the way as I did His daily will, developed myself for His service, and stayed surrendered.

God has allowed me to do far more and serve Him in more ways than I ever dreamed! God's will is the best!

DRAW
Me NEARER
Today in...

"I am Thine, O Lord, I have heard Thy voice,
And it told Thy love to me;
But I long to rise in the arms of faith,
And be closer drawn to Thee."

Trust the Driver

By Marsha Leto

Casting all your care upon him, for he careth for you.

I Peter 5:7

Does anyone else get a little nervous driving on the interstate when there are tractor-trailers to the left and right of you? At times, I have felt like I could get sandwiched between the two. This was the scenario a few weeks ago. Thankfully, I was not driving, but I was still feeling quite a bit of anxiety. My husband could tell by looking at me that I was a bit uneasy. He reached over and patted my hand and said, "Sweetheart, trust the driver."

At first, my mind raced. "Trust the driver?" I thought. That is easy for you to say. Do you know how fast we are going? Do you see all these tractor-trailers? Why is that car zooming in and out of traffic? Why are there red lights ahead? All these scenarios popped into my mind. How could I possibly trust the driver! Then I stopped ... and looked at my husband.

Slowly, the thought process started working. I needed to have a little talk with myself. I started thinking ... He has kept me safe for all these years. He has driven thousands of miles without an accident. He does have his CDL. He has driven tractor-trailers and buses for years.

107

"And we know that all things work together for good to them that love God, to them who are the called according to his purpose."

- Romans 8:28

He is a safe driver. So, why am I worried? Yes, my husband is right, I just need to trust the driver! I smiled, took his hand, and said, "You are right. I do need to just trust the driver."

Let us relate this story to the Christian life. Who should be the driver of our lives? We all know the answer to that question – God. But so many times we hop from the passenger seat to the driver's seat because we think we know best. Situations come up and instead of praying about those situations, we choose to worry. When I was riding with my husband, I thought the driver with the CDL and many years of experience did not see what I saw. Not only did he see it, but he saw it miles before I did. How foolish of me to think that he needed my expertise and driving suggestions. We can act the same way with God. He created us, He wants what is best for us, and He knows us better than anyone, but we still have trouble trusting Him. Trust means "to have confidence, a reliance or resting of the mind on the integrity, veracity, justice, friendship, or other sound principle of another person." We can trust God. We can have confidence in God. God already knows what is going to happen and what is happening in our lives. I Peter 5:7, "Casting all your care upon him, for he careth for you." I must admit there are times I struggle with trusting God. I have done a few things that have helped me in this area.

1. I have a serious talk with myself. It is okay to talk to yourself, occasionally. I have asked myself these questions: Has God ever failed me? Does God love me? Does God want what is best for me? The point of asking these questions is to put myself back in the passenger seat. Sometimes ladies do not want to trust because they want to control. It is either one or the other, but not both. A happy life is trusting. The anxiety-filled life is control.

2. I remember what He has done in the past. I can look in my prayer journal at past answers to prayer. I am encouraged by the past prayers that have been answered.

3. I look up verses and put them in places where I can read them. The verses encourage me and remind me that God is faithful and can be trusted. Proverbs 3:5-6, "Trust in the Lord with all thine heart; and lean not to thine own understanding. In all thy ways acknowledge him, and he shall direct thy paths." We know the verses Proverbs 3:5-6. We even have it highlighted in our Bibles, but do we believe them?

4. I pray more often about the need I have. James 5:16B, "The effectual fervent prayer of a righteous man availeth much."

I am not sure where you are in this journey of trusting God – but you can trust Him. He knows what is best. Trusting God gives us peace and confidence in His plan. Romans 8:28, "And we know that all things work together for good to them that love God, to them who are the called according to his purpose."

There have been times that I have struggled with trusting God. Unfortunately, those times were filled with worry and fear. I can never get those days back that I spent worrying. You have heard it before, but it is a good reminder – "Worry is like a rocking chair: it gives you something to do, but never gets you anywhere."

DRAW *Me* NEARER

Today in...

"*I am Thine, O Lord, I have heard Thy voice,*
And it told Thy love to me;
But I long to rise in the arms of faith,
And be closer drawn to Thee."

Purple Paint:
A Lesson in Obedience

By Sarah Russell

Children, obey your parents in the Lord: for this is right.

Ephesians 6:1

Philippians 2:5-8, "Let this mind be in you, which was also in Christ Jesus: Who, being in the form of God, thought it not robbery to be equal with God: But made himself of no reputation, and took upon him the form of a servant, and was made in the likeness of men: And being found in fashion as a man, he humbled himself, and became obedient unto death, even the death of the cross."

"When obedience to God contradicts what I think will give me pleasure, let me ask myself if I love Him." – Elisabeth Elliot

"A whole lot of what we call 'struggling' is simply delayed obedience." – Elisabeth Elliot.

One summer's day my four-year-old daughter came to me with a box of paints and asked if we could paint a picture for someone. A sweet thought, but I was a bit busy at the time so I said, "Not right now. Maybe later today. Go and put the paint away for now." Then I left the room and went back to my housework.

A short time later, my sweet girl came to me with a look of guilt, her paints in hand. Her shirt was all wet from her attempts to wash away the evidence of her disobedience. There, with downcast eyes, she confessed that she had opened the paint, made a mess, and tried to clean it up. I finished cleaning her up and sent her to wait for me in her room for further "discussion" on the matter. Then I went to the kitchen to further assess the messy situation.

There was no evidence of paint where my daughter had been sitting. But in the next seat over sat her little sister, covered with purple paint! With a bit of exasperation, I cleaned her up and changed her clothes. And then we finished our "discussion" about obedience with the two of them.

Later as I sat pondering the seemingly funny situation and mess, the Lord put this thought in my heart as a reminder.

At times, as God's child, He tells me not to do something, or tells me to stop and wait patiently until He gives me the go-ahead. When we are obedient children we say, "Yes sir!" We wait patiently, we stop in obedience, and we listen to our loving Father, for He knows best! But at times we are disobedient. We push ahead of our Father. We go ahead and do the thing He told us not to do. "How bad could it be? He's let me do it before. Why should I be patient? What could happen?"

Disobedience is sin no matter how big or small.

When my little girl disobeyed and opened her paint, it wasn't in her plan to get messy. And it never occurred to her that her younger sister would join her or that purple paint would be all over the place.

But isn't that just the way sin is? We don't plan on our simple disobedience getting us messy. It's just a little thing in our eyes.

And of course, no one else could possibly be affected by our decision, right?

My daughter didn't get very messy with her paint. And she did a good job cleaning herself up, considering her age. But there was still evidence of her disobedience. There was still a little bit of paint on her clothes and hands. I knew she had disobeyed without her saying a word. Just as when I disobey what my Father has said in His Word or through His Spirit, He knows I disobeyed before I ever confess. I may try to clean up my mess and fix the problem, but eventually, I have to go to my Father and confess that I disobeyed. I made a mess of things again. And though He gives me a "discussion," He also washes me in His love and His chastisement reminds me that I am His child. I can't stay in my mess. It must be cleaned up, but He still loves me.

But you know the thing about this messy story that touches my heart the most? My daughter's disobedience affected more than just herself. Her mess went beyond herself. Her decision to disobey brought about the choice of someone else to sin along with her. Someone else followed her example. And her sister's mess was far worse than her own. A mess that she couldn't even begin to clean up herself.

So what's the lesson here? People are watching you. People are following your example ... a sister in Christ, an unsaved coworker, perhaps your very own children. Your disobedience will, without a doubt, affect others. When we choose disobedience in our lives, someone may be right behind us following our path of destruction. The thoughts some may have could be, "If Sarah did it, it must be fine."

"If she watches that TV show, reads that book, or acts with that sort of attitude it surely can't be wrong."

We must be so careful to not become a stumbling block to another soul along the way — saved or lost.

We will give an account of our disobedience and its influence on others. Our complete obedience to our Father is the least we can do for Him! And Christ is the supreme Example of true obedience. Philippians 2:5-8 reminds us that He was obedient even unto death! And the effect of His obedience is our salvation. What obedience!

So how is your obedience today? Are we submitted and obedient to God's Word? Or are we in disobedience, negatively affecting our friends and families' choices? Are we following Christ's example of obedience to the very end? Or are we choosing our "purple paint"? Let's choose to live in sweet obedience today, my friend! It truly is the very best way to live!

There is no life like an obedient Christian's life.

DRAW Me NEARER

Today in ...

"I am Thine, O Lord, I have heard Thy voice,
And it told Thy love to me;
But I long to rise in the arms of faith,
And be closer drawn to Thee."

Our Spiritual Garden - Growing in Christ

By Cherith Shiflett

"But other fell into good ground, and brought forth fruit, some an hundredfold, some sixtyfold, some thirtyfold."

Matthew 13:8

Spring is one of my favorite times of the year. I love to watch everything come back to life after a long, cold winter. I enjoy the warm weather, gentle breezes, pretty flowers, and the birds. This year I enjoyed planting little seeds and watching them grow. Several times as I watered and checked on them, I thought of the spiritual applications of a garden. I think the Lord loves gardens. He created the Garden of Eden for the beginning of life, and nearing the end of His life, He prayed in a garden – the garden of Gethsemane.

So, what are some spiritual lessons we can learn from a garden?

Soil – the soil you plant in is important. We learn this from the parable of the sower.

Matthew 13:4-8 describes the different places a seed can fall, "And when he sowed, some seeds fell by the way side, and the fowls came and devoured them up: Some fell upon stony places, where they had not much earth: and forthwith they sprung up, because they had no deepness of earth: And when the sun was up, they were scorched; and because they had no root, they withered away. And some fell among thorns; and the thorns sprung up, and choked them: But other fell into good ground, and brought forth fruit, some an hundredfold, some sixtyfold, some thirtyfold."

A seed has to have "good ground" to bring forth fruit. Plants have to have a good foundation to start their growth and develop roots. This can be a picture of salvation – when you hear the Gospel, accept the Lord as your Saviour, and begin to be grounded in Him. He is our ultimate foundation. It all begins with Him. Don't be the one who has the seed fall on stony ground, thorny ground, or by the way side. If you haven't accepted God's free gift of salvation, do it today! Start your foundation for spiritual growth.

Sunlight – When I read the back of the seedling packets, I always get nervous about too much sunlight or too little sunlight or what if I need to get a growth light? ... And then I just threw some seeds in a pot and set them outside my front door. And guess what? They sprouted perfectly. They got the perfect amount of sunlight. I think it's amazing God knows exactly what each little flower, each little blade of grass needs for this season, and He lovingly takes care of each little bud.

Luke 12: 27-28, "Consider the lilies how they grow; they toil not, they spin not; and yet I say unto you, that Solomon in all his glory was not arrayed like one of these. If then God so clothe the grass, which is today in the field, and tomorrow is cast into the oven; how much more will he clothe you, O ye of little faith?"

We overthink and over complicate needs that God has ALREADY taken care of. If God takes the time to make sure a lily has the necessary components to grow, don't you think He will give you everything you need to grow?

Water–– In order to grow, plants have to have water. As Christians, we are the same. We have to have the water of the Word in order to grow. You can give a plant all the nutrients, fertilizer, good soil, and sunlight you want, but if you don't have water, it will die. So many times, Christians wonder why they're dead spiritually, possibly even doubting their salvation, but when you ask them if they're reading their Bible, the answer is, "It's been awhile." Of course you're doubting! Of course you're dying. There is no water being applied.

Ephesians 5:26, "That he might sanctify and cleanse it with the washing of water by the word."

The only way to grow, to live holy, and cleanse our hearts is by the Water of the Word. Don't just read your Proverbs for the day and be done – actually meditate and give your seed a good watering. We want to be well-watered, not barely hanging on because we get water once a week.

Weeds – Whenever you have growth, you're going to have weeds. I remember as a child pulling weeds out of my mom's flower gardens for what seemed like hours! I remember wishing we could just leave them there! But weeds choke plants. They create an atmosphere that

121

is impossible for growth, and if you don't take care of them quickly, they completely overrun a garden. Check your garden. Are there weeds of gossip? Discontentment? Bitterness? Complacency? So many different "weeds" can pop up so quickly. We have to address it and pull that weed out. As a child, I remember times I would pull and pull on a weed and it just wasn't coming out. We would have to bring in reinforcements – a spade or even a big shovel. If you can't get the weed out on your own, seek reinforcements. Talk to your Pastor's wife or a Christian mentor. Get that weed out before it chokes your growth and overtakes your garden.

In conclusion, I always think of my mom when I think of gardening. She has the most beautiful flower bed, arches, greenery, and gardens. She works hard every year preparing, pruning, clearing out weeds and planting. And then she is able to come out in the mornings and enjoy the fruit of her labor and spend time with the Lord in her garden.

We are the gardeners of our hearts. We have all the necessary components to have beautiful growth, but it takes work and care.

How is your spiritual garden? Is it overrun or dead? Or is it a beautiful testimony of new life in Christ?

DRAW Me NEARER

Today in ...

"*I am Thine, O Lord, I have heard Thy voice,*
And it told Thy love to me;
But I long to rise in the arms of faith,
And be closer drawn to Thee."

Be a Jochebed

By Beverley Wells

And the woman conceived, and bare a son:
and when she saw him that he was a goodly child,
she hid him three months.

Exodus 2:2

Good day, my sweet friend. As you read this article, I pray that you are having a great day in the Lord. As we approach another Mother's Day, my thoughts have been going back to a story in the Old Testament focusing on Moses and his sweet mother Jochebed – the setting being one of a political reign, worldly culture, and a great time of despair. Sounds somewhat familiar to the days that we are living in.

As we read the story of Moses and the detailed watch care of his mother during his early years of life, there is hope of God's protecting hand on our very own children. No doubt when she knew that she was expecting another child, a precious gift from God, Pharaoh was already extracting tiny little lives in his anticipation to annihilate the small children that he suspected would seek his throne. What fear she must have had knowing that her child's life was in great danger.

With that being said, we must realize that there is one looking to extract our small children from us and the truth of the gospel.

125

Jochebed gives us a great example of the responsibilities of being a mother. As she heard the screams of many mothers around her, as they cried out in desperation, pleading for the life of their children, she was doing her best to keep Moses hidden from the evil influences that were seeking to destroy him. How she did this is beyond my comprehension. How do you keep an infant from crying? If you have had a newborn, then you know what I am talking about. They cry in the midnight hours when all around is quiet and sleeping. They cry when they are hungry, when they are wet, and sometimes for no reason at all. She kept him quiet for three months. This had to be God!

I imagine during her nine months of pregnancy, she was devising a plan of how to protect her son, giving great attention to the preparations that were needed ahead.

If you are a young mother with small children, have you made it a point to devise a plan of protection for your children? This is so crucial for their future to protect them from the dangers that lie ahead. Be their shield, guard, and defender! They are not yet equipped for the battle. They cannot see the enemy before them. They do not have the strength to defend themselves.

Prepare the way! Pray for them! Position them in the way! Place them in His care!

The task was not easy, but she knew there was a greater purpose. She had a vision for him. The perfect plan was to weave a basket and to cover it in slime and pitch (tar-like substance) that would be waterproof.

She placed growing Moses in it and sent him out into the elements of the world. She had been very thorough in her preparations.

Perhaps putting it through tests to make sure the job was complete. We don't know if she had to make several baskets until she made the perfect one or not. Her careful attention to details was also observed by Miriam (Moses' sister) as she was instructed on her part of the plan. Jochebed's focus did not just include one child but all her children. Each was given instructions to do the job that needed to be done.

How wise were the choices made by Jochebed! Her trust was in the unseen hand of the Lord. Her faith had to be in the God of Israel. Was it easy? Absolutely not!

How sure are we to let go and let God? If we will be as Jochebed, then we too can press on and know that God is in control. We must trust God with the in-between parts of the journey. Knowing that this is not to hurt us but to develop us. To experience a Jochebed life, we must walk a life consecrated unto our Lord – obedient to His Word even in the darkest of times.

How interested are we in being used to develop God-honoring children that will walk in His way?

Moses was influenced greatly in his young years and because of his childhood training, he was used mightily. The formative years are of the greatest importance, for it is then that one's character is developed. We as parents have a crucial role during these short years.

How would you like to see your child's life play out? Successful in Christ or selfish in quest? One can only imagine how everything played out. It was Jochebed that bore the burden of standing post to guard and guide. As she prepared the ark of bulrushes, covering every nook and cranny with slime and pitch, I'm sure you could hear the prayers to Jehovah to protect this goodly child. Jochebed had, without reserve, given him into the hands of her Lord.

We must do the same. Resolve to do all the Word instructs us to do as mothers – dying daily to yourself and allowing Christ to live through us. When we live as Christ, we can step back and let His purpose be fulfilled. Never retreat though the pressures are unbearable. There is strength in the Lord! The rewards are unmeasurable!

Be a Jochebed....

Prepare the way!

- Deuteronomy 6:5-9, II Timothy 1:5, Hebrews 11:23-29

Pray for them!

- Proverbs 1:7, Matthew 19:14, Isaiah 11:2, II Thessalonians 3:2-3

Position in the way!

- Psalm 1:1, Esther 4:14, Daniel 1:8-12, Proverbs 22:6

Post yourself as a guard!

- Ezekiel 33, Isaiah 62:6

Place them in His hands!

- (Samuel was placed in God's hands) I Samuel 3:1-10

Praise Him for His promises!

- Psalm 1:1

DRAW Me NEARER

Today in...

"I am Thine, O Lord, I have heard Thy voice,
And it told Thy love to me;
But I long to rise in the arms of faith,
And be closer drawn to Thee."

Hey, Zeruiah, the 'Maintenance Required' Light is On!

By Kim Thompson

This is a faithful saying, and these things I will that thou affirm constantly, that they which have believed in God might be careful to maintain good works. These things are good and profitable unto men.... And let ours also learn to maintain good works for necessary uses, that they be not unfruitful.

Titus 3:8, 14

I've read the Bible through many times, and I do confess there were times that I read it in a lazy manner. I zipped through genealogies and chose not to spend a second longer than necessary on the pronunciation of names such as Sabtecha, Naphtuhim, Pathrusim, etc. (My husband has such a great sense of humor! He would have enjoyed coming up with nicknames for those guys!) I would have read the name Zeruiah many times before I ever even realized she was a woman! Now, as I proceed with this blog, please understand I'm taking liberty with my thoughts about Zeruiah. The Holy Scriptures do not give us many details about who she was emotionally, mentally, and spiritually. We do, however, know a tad bit more about her offspring. I'd like to take a look at this mother Zeruiah.

131

The name Zeruiah means Balsam from Jehovah – what a sweet sentiment! With a great brood of guys in the house, (King) David being the youngest boy, maybe her mother was thrilled to have this sweet daughter to help out with the domestic chores and to experience constant female companionship in the home. Whatever the case, the meaning of her name signifies a great start. The fact that her name is mentioned around 25 times in the Bible must also mean she was a woman of prominence. Curiosity compels me to ask many questions: Was David her little sidekick back in the day? Or was she the classic bossy big sis? Was she proud of David when he told of how the Lord enabled him to kill the giant Goliath? (I've smiled at the different filial scenarios that might have taken place in the house of Jesse.) In the end, though, did grandparents, parents, or brothers spoil this Balsam? Was there a point in her childhood or married life that made this balsamic (healing) woman bitter?

At some point, Zeruiah marries and has 3 sons. I Chronicles 2:16 "... And the sons of Zeruiah; Abishai, and Joab, and Asahel, three." We know that Joab, Abishai, and Asahel were men of action! If a job needed done, these were your guys! However, these "sons of Zeruiah" grieved the heart of King David, the authority of the day – and after reading I Samuel 13:14, we know that the heart of David sought to align itself with the heart of God! Thus something was askew in the lives of these sons. Did Mom Zeruiah flippantly fulfill her role as a mother? My hope is that Zeruiah reared her children with the philosophy that my own mother possessed – "Maintain good works" in words and actions. Maintenance in our daily lives keeps the heart right.

My maternal grandmother, for a time, turned her back on her Christian upbringing. She married out of the Lord's will, and by the time my mother was born, my maternal grandfather was an alcoholic. With a thankful heart, my mom will testify that she didn't experience the harshness that her older siblings lived with with this drunken father. My mother only remembers being surrounded by a godly, repentant mother and such godly grandparents! (I loved my great grandfather– what a precious man! He was a soul winner back in the day before that particular word had been invented!) My mother is now 78 years old, and I'm so happy and grateful that she maintained good works in her words and actions, even when her heart must have been screaming at and even demanding her to scrap the maintenance – it's just not worth it. My mom's journey has not been easy - my father passed away at the age of 40 due to lymphoma. Mom was a widow at the age of 33 with five kids – my baby sister was exactly one month old when Dad passed. My mother is my earthly example that a Heavenly Father is real. I know now from our adult conversations that there were moments when she ignored the spiritual Maintenance Required light, but she eventually made the necessary reparations in her heart and spirit.

After my own salvation and as I continued to age and mature, I realized that what was good for my precious, loving mother was good for me!

It was time for me to learn to maintain good works so that I wouldn't be unfruitful! As I write this, I'm motivated more than ever to maintain good works. Today, we're living some crazy "woke" times.

As I think of Zeruiah, I can't help but assume she chose to ignore the "Maintenance Required" light and that she chose to selfishly execute her own way and will ... I believe the lives of her sons show that! "And I am this day weak, though anointed king; and these men the sons of Zeruiah be too hard for me ...." (II Samuel 3:39) "What have I to do with you, ye sons of Zeruiah?" (II Samuel 16:10) These sons lacked loyalty; these sons softened the importance of full submission to God-given leadership, and these sons made their own agenda their final authority. Oh, if only Momma Zeruiah had been more aware, heeded the signs, and been "careful to maintain good works," we might have read in the eternal Scriptures about hers also maintaining "good works for necessary uses, that they be not unfruitful." Instead, we see the tragic end, the "car crash" if you will, of the lives of her sons. Don't be weary in well doing, sisters! The effort and energy required for the daily maintenance of one's heart and life is truly easier in the long run than the effort and energy demanded for the salvaging of a totaled life.

DRAW
Me NEARER
Today in ...

"I am Thine, O Lord, I have heard Thy voice,
And it told Thy love to me;
But I long to rise in the arms of faith,
And be closer drawn to Thee."

Renew My Spirit

By Rikki Beth Poindexter

Create in me a clean heart, O God; and renew a right spirit within me.

Psalm 51:10

Renew means "to resume after an interruption; to renovate; to rebuild; to repair; to revive; to restore to freshness." We renew things that are important to us and things that require renewing. Some people choose to renew their wedding vows. On the other hand, we have to renew our driver's license. What about our most important relationship: the one with the Lord? Does it need renewing? I know mine does from time to time. Sometimes it gets stagnant, or I begin to drift.

Most of us know that Psalm 51 is David's psalm of repentance. He is, if you will, renewing his relationship with God. The relationship has been interrupted; it needs repairing. It needs a restoration to freshness. David has sinned with Bathsheeba, has had her husband killed, and in this Psalm is getting right with God after a time of interruption.

For us to renew our relationship with the Lord, we will need to spend time with Him. This whole psalm is a talk that David has with the Lord. If your relationship needs some freshness, spend some time with Him! Don't neglect your daily time with the Lord. We will find ourselves in a mess. David did not wake up one day and decide to commit adultery and then have a man killed. Oh no! Rest assured, this was a gradual process that probably began with him missing his time with the Lord. Don't miss it.

Everything rests on our daily walk with the Lord. If we are missing our time with Him, we must identify the time wasters and deal with them. Make no mistake, we all have the same amount of time and we are all busy!

I get enamored with folks who think they are the only ones who are busy. However, we make time for the things that are important to us. Make time to read your Bible, do some studying of it, and talk to the Lord daily. If you have no desire for that, find out why. Are you even truly saved? Saved people love the Word! If you are saved and have no desire for the Word, what has taken the desire from you? Get "that" out of your life or in its proper place.

David deals with his transgressions in this psalm. Psalm 51:1, "Have mercy upon me, O God, according to thy lovingkindness: according unto the multitude of thy tender mercies blot out my transgressions."

If my relationship with the Lord is not what I wish it were, maybe I need to clean up some things. Maybe there are some things I need to confess and forsake. I must keep a short list with the Lord. I want to be able to talk to Him whenever I want or need to. To have that open line of communication, I must stay clean.

Psalm 66:18, "If I regard iniquity in my heart, the Lord will not hear me." Sometimes, we are well aware of our transgressions and have not repented; other times we may have forgotten that the Lord dealt with us over them; then there is the case where we haven't been dealt with about a particular sin. Whatever the situation, one of the best ways to renew our most important relationship is to keep the transgression list short.

Our treasures (the things that are important to us) need to be the same as God's. If my relationship with the Lord needs some freshness restored to it, maybe I should check to see that my treasures are the same as His. A clean heart and a right spirit are what David has asked for; these things were important to the Lord.

Do our treasures line up with His? How important is His Word? How important is assembling with the church family we are a part of? (I'm convinced if church attendance sheets were kept, many people would not believe them when they were handed theirs. They would argue that they didn't miss that much church.)

How important are His people to us? What about the souls of men? Do we give back to the Lord in tithes and offerings? Do you give for your church to be able to support missionaries? Follow the money trail in your checkbooks or banking app to find out what your treasures are. Do we pay more for our cell phones in a month than we give to missions? Is serving important to you? Our service sure is important to Him. Do our treasures line up with His?

To renew my relationship with Jesus, I must renew my thankfulness to Him! Our Lord loves for us to thank Him, to praise Him for His mighty acts and His wonderful works.

Psalm 150:2, "Praise him for his mighty acts: praise him according to his excellent greatness."

Psalm 92:1 tells us it is a good thing to give thanks unto the Lord. He loves thankful people, and we understand that because most of us do too. We don't mind at all doing things for those who will be thankful! I don't know about you, but I want my relationship with the Lord to be fresh! I want to put the work and effort in to make sure it is in good shape. I want to have my priorities in line and get my time in with Him every day. I want to keep a short list with the Lord, a clean heart, and an open line of communication. I want to make sure my treasures line up with His. He deserves my thankfulness and praise.

DRAW *Me* NEARER
Today in...

"*I am Thine, O Lord, I have heard Thy voice,*
And it told Thy love to me;
But I long to rise in the arms of faith,
And be closer drawn to Thee."

Rest in the Lord

By Susan Hutchens

Come unto me, all ye that labor and are heavy laden, and I will give you rest.

Matthew 11:28

Rest. Do you love it? Work is necessary and valuable, and play is good too, but we also need rest. For some people, rest is a necessary evil — they only rest when they are forced to. For others, rest comes more easily (maybe too easily!). They tend to pace themselves so they don't get overwhelmed. But all of us come to a point when we need physical rest, and the same is true spiritually.

We see this in the biblical account of two sisters, Mary and Martha, in Luke 10:38-42. Martha is running around doing all the things in preparation for Jesus and His disciples to eat with the family, and she looks out and sees Mary sitting at the feet of Jesus — when there's work to be done! If you've ever been busy working and found someone who should be helping you decidedly not helping, you know how Martha felt! When she complained to Jesus, He was quick to point out that Martha was careful (or full of care) and troubled about many things, but Mary had chosen the one thing that was needful — sitting at His feet. How could Mary be resting when there was so much to do? There are three events in the Bible that feature Mary and her family, and every time we see Mary, she is at the feet of Jesus. Let's take a look.

First, we learn that Mary was content resting in God's provision of fellowship with Him. Luke 10:42 says that Mary had chosen the one thing that was needful, and that was sitting at the feet of Jesus. God has graciously given us the one thing we need: fellowship with Him.

I know you hear it again and again: the way to have fellowship with God is by reading His Word, praying regularly, and keeping short accounts with God about our sin. The amazing thing? God wants this fellowship with us and to give us rest! He knows we will get tired, careful and troubled about many things, and He offers us rest. It's the most needful thing (Matthew 11:28).

Notice that Mary had chosen to be content with fellowship with Jesus: "Mary hath chosen that good part...." Much of the Christian life is made up of choices. We choose to read the Bible, pray, witness, react with grace, forgive, and be kind. Likewise, fellowship with God is our choice (Revelation 3:20). He doesn't force us to fellowship with Him. Are you choosing to fellowship with Jesus, or are you letting life happen and hoping that you'll develop a close relationship with the Lord? Unfortunately, resting in God doesn't just happen; you have to choose to rest in Him.

Life is busy, and as Christian wives, mothers, daughters, sisters, friends, and church members, we can easily be overwhelmed by all we have to do.

But God invites us to be content in His provision of fellowship with Him. Like Mary, take time to sit at His feet by reading His Word and talking to Him in prayer.

Next in our study of Mary, we see that she was consoled in her grief because she was resting in God's compassion. Mary was free to pour out her heart to Him in her grief: "... Lord, if thou hadst been here, my brother had not died" (John 11:32). Even when we know God's promises, there are times when we just need to pour out our hearts to Him. When Mary did exactly that, Jesus didn't get angry with her or chastise her for her grief. He understood her grief and wept with her (John 11:35). What a thought, that Jesus would weep with us! We have further comfort that Jesus is not a high priest who cannot be touched with the feelings of our infirmities (Hebrews 4:15-16). He knows and He cares about what we go through!

Are you going through something today that brings you to Jesus' feet? He knows, and He cares, and He doesn't get upset with you for your grief! Remember the promises of God and trust Him. Be confident, and rest in His compassion!

Finally, the last time we see Mary of Bethany in Scripture, she is comfortable resting in His presence (John 12:1-7). At that time and in that culture, women were not seen as equal with men. They would have been serving the meal, but not sitting with the men listening to a teacher visiting in the home. But Mary comfortably sat at His feet to hear Him. A man probably wouldn't have bothered himself with a woman's grief, but Mary wept at Jesus' feet and poured out her heart to Him when her brother died. And Jesus wept with her. A woman would not have let down her hair in the presence of men; that would have been considered immodest. But Mary was comfortable enough with Jesus to wipe his feet with her hair. Mary could find rest with her dearest friend, Jesus.

Jesus wants us to be comfortable with Him in the sense that we are comfortable with a family member (Romans 8:15). My husband and

I have hosted many preachers and missionaries in our home, and let me tell you, I don't get completely comfortable with visitors in my home! I don't go and put on my nightgown and robe after supper and lie on the couch reading. We talk about many things, but we don't generally talk about our deepest thoughts and feelings. I fix "nice" food, not beans and potatoes or peanut butter and jelly sandwiches. On the other hand, when I'm with my husband, I relax. I get comfortable in the evening; we eat plain old food that we enjoy; we talk about the innermost thoughts of our hearts. I'm intimately familiar with my husband, so I am comfortable in his presence.

I want to know Jesus so well that I can rest comfortably in His presence.

I can tell you that there is sweet rest in the Lord Jesus, in His provision, in His compassion, in His presence. I've learned that, just as He reached out to offer salvation, He also reaches out to offer rest. Nothing can separate me from God's love. I can come into His presence as a daughter. I can rest in the Lord!

Can you rest in the Lord? Are you content in God's provision of fellowship? Are you comforted by His compassion for you? Are you comfortable with Jesus? Can you rest in His love for you? Thank Him for rest, and continue to have close fellowship with Him. And if you have trouble resting in the Lord, get familiar with Him through His Word and prayer, and you will begin finding rest for your soul!

DRAW
Me NEARER
Today in ...

"I am Thine, O Lord, I have heard Thy voice,
And it told Thy love to me;
But I long to rise in the arms of faith,
And be closer drawn to Thee."

Lessons Learned in a Trial

By Lois Van Zee

But he knoweth the way that I take: when he hath tried me, I shall come forth as gold.

Job 23:10

Trials are hard, but oh so cleansing for those who trust God through them!

Watching our son and daughter-in-love go through this trial was amazing and increased my husband's and my faith. Jamison was born six weeks early due to him having a really bad case of cardiomyopathy. Our daughter-in-love was born with it also – hers was not as bad; with medicine, she's been able to live a normal life – and the doctors weren't sure if it would affect any of their children. They chose to trust God with having children. Jamison was their first child and our first grandchild. We ended up having to let him go as there was nothing more the doctors could try after he fought so hard for three months in the hospital. By the way, after Jamison, God chose to bless our son and daughter-in-love with two more children.

The verse below was the verse that my daughter-in-love claimed during this time.

Psalm 139:14, "I will praise thee; for I am fearfully and wonderfully made: marvelous are thy works; and that my soul knoweth right well."

God gave me this devotion two weeks after Jamison's death and gave me the peace that I so desperately needed. Things I learned and claimed through our grandson's short time on earth.

1. I have learned God is in control of everything. (He is sovereign.)

He knew, formed, and allowed Jamison to have a heart that did not work normally. Even though I specifically prayed, knowing that Mommy had a weak heart and it was a possibility that he would also, that God would allow him to have a healthy heart. God did not choose to do my bidding because of a greater good that He knew would come out of this defect. We may never know what that is, but we can be assured that God is in control and we have His promise that He will never leave us nor forsake us. A couple of verses that God gave me during this time are Psalm 139:17 and 18, "How precious also are thy thoughts unto me, O God! How great is the sum of them! If I should count them, they are more In number than the sand: when I awake, I am still with thee." He cares when we hurt. Psalm 34:18 says, "The Lord is nigh unto them that are of a broken heart; and saveth such as be of a contrite spirit."

2. I have learned when we don't agree with God and rail at Him, we are as one of the foolish women.

During this time God showed me Job 2:10 – "... What? shall we receive good at the hand of God, and shall we not receive evil?" Job says this to his wife when she tells him to curse God and die. God is not a respecter of persons. He brings into our lives what is needed for us to grow spiritually and to be made into who He needs us to become for Him. There was one point during this ordeal when I didn't think God was taking care of my kids, and I kind of got upset with Him. Later, I humbly had to go to God and ask for forgiveness for my thoughts, because, to my chagrin, several days later, I found out God had everything under control and was taking care of my kids better than I ever could imagine, which, by the way, He has promised to do: Matthew 6:33, "But seek ye first the kingdom of God and his righteousness and all these things shall be added unto you." Key words there are "but seek." Don't expect God to take care of you if you haven't first been seeking Him.

3. I have learned God uses us as it pleases Him.

Hebrews 13:21 says, "Make you perfect (or complete) in every good work to do His will, working in you that which is well-pleasing in his sight, through Jesus Christ; to whom be glory for ever and ever. Amen." As Christian ladies, we should want God to work in and through us what is well pleasing in His sight knowing that God knows the beginning from the end. We must trust and believe that He doesn't do anything for our hurt but only for our good. Romans 8:28, "And we know that all things work together for good to them that love God, to them who are the called according to his purpose." And why does He allow trials into our lives? So that we may be conformed to the image of His Son, as verse 29 says in the same chapter.

4. I have learned not to be afraid of bad news.

Psalm 112:7, "He [talking about the righteous man] shall not be afraid of evil tidings: his heart is fixed, trusting in the Lord." We must be so in tune with God that we don't question His motives; we automatically trust in Him and His ways. As Job said in Job 13:15a, "Though he slay me, yet will I trust in him," and in Proverbs 3:5, 6 it says, "Trust in the Lord with all thine heart; and lean not unto thine own understanding. In all thy ways acknowledge him, and he shall direct thy paths."

5. I have learned God is faithful.

No matter the outcome of our trials one thing we do know and can come out of it with is that God is faithful. II Thessalonians 3:3, "But the Lord is faithful, who shall stablish you, and keep you from evil." As I did a search on the word "evil" and went to several other passages, as far as I could understand, the evil talks of Satan. If we are Christians, we should be thankful that nothing in this world matters except that God is faithful to bring us to heaven no matter what happens here on this earth.

6. I have learned God is good.

Psalm 73:1 says, "Truly God is good to Israel, even to such as are of a clean heart." And again in Psalm 107:8, "Oh that men would praise the Lord for his goodness, and for his wonderful works to the children of men!" Here is another favorite verse of mine about the Lord's goodness - Psalm 34:8, "O taste and see that the Lord is good: blessed is the man that trusteth in him." I can say no matter the outcome of the trial, God is always good. Again, if you are a blood bought child of God, no matter what happens here on this earth you are going to Heaven. Now that should put a smile on our faces and joy into our hearts. Praise God during trials for finding you worthy to be used by Him.

DRAW Me NEARER

Today in...

"I am Thine, O Lord, I have heard Thy voice,
And it told Thy love to me;
But I long to rise in the arms of faith,
And be closer drawn to Thee."

The Strength of the Lord

By Anja Meyer

I can do all things through Christ which strengtheneth me.

Philippians 4:13

The fact that I studied Maths at university, proves how much I enjoy the order, precision, and rule-following of this subject. So, when my friend spoke of this formula, if you will, in the Scriptures, I was naturally intrigued. It follows a progression between verses, and it meant a lot to me to study this out.

As wives, mothers, daughters, sisters, and friends, we often pray and long for the strength of the Lord. It could be worries and fears, significant loss, financial or relationship stress or physical weakness, or weariness that press us – we find that we need strength from the Lord to walk through it to the glory of God.

Look at Philippians 4:13 with me: "I can do all things through Christ which strengtheneth me."

Paul explains in the previous verse how he has gone through a range of difficult trials, but he has learned, and knows for sure, that the Lord will give him the strength he needs. He is confident that he can go through it with this strength from the Lord.

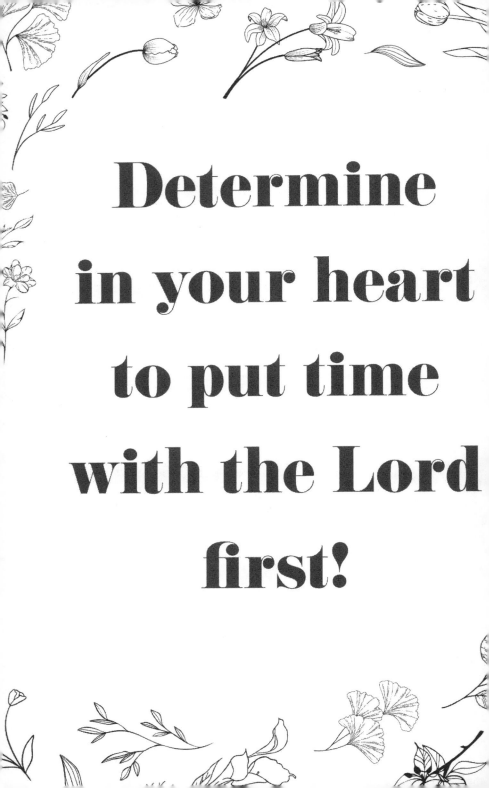

Determine in your heart to put time with the Lord first!

So, how do we get this strength of the Lord that we so desperately need?

Follow me on to the last part of Nehemiah 8:10 - "... for the joy of the Lord is your strength."

Despite tremendous intimidation and hindrance, Nehemiah oversaw the rebuilding of the walls of Jerusalem, and finally, it was completed. The children of Israel were settling back into their land. At the start of Chapter Eight, the people congregated before the water gate and asked Ezra, the scribe, to read from the law of Moses to them. They desired to hear what the Lord had commanded Israel. After Ezra had read to the people from morning until midday, and several men had explained to them what Ezra read, the people worshipped the Lord in tears. Nehemiah then instructed the people to have a feast, because this intense joy that they received from hearing and understanding the words of the Lord was their strength.

This leads me to the middle part of the next verse, Psalm 16:11 — ... in thy presence is fullness of joy...."

The joy, which is the strength of the Lord that we so desperately need, is found in the presence of the Lord. Spending time with the Lord can be tricky in a busy household season full of little children to care for, a season of illness, or a season of extra demands on our time from outside the home. Dear friend, we cannot let the precious time of communion with our Lord fall by the wayside. I have been guilty of this and suffered the loss of my joy, which is my strength.

Determine in your heart to put time with the Lord first, hear His Words, understand them, and spend time in prayer with Him.

So, how exactly do we approach the Lord? Psalm 100 explains clearly:

Verse 2 – "... come before his presence with singing ...."

Verse 4 – "Enter into his gates with thanksgiving, and into his courts with praise: be thankful unto him, and bless his name."

We come into the Lord's presence with thankfulness in our hearts and praise on our lips. This directs our thoughts and minds to the wonderful Heavenly Father He is. It reminds us of how able and willing He is to equip, enable, and encourage us in whatever trial we're facing. This brings joy to our hearts which cannot be quenched by any circumstance we find ourselves in.

Finally, we can function in the strength of the Lord as Paul described in Philippians 4!

Please do not forget this mathematical formula:

singing + thanksgiving + praise -> the presence of the Lord -> fullness of joy = the strength of the Lord

Dear friend, we serve a wonderful God. May you live in His strength.

Psalm 100:5 – "For the Lord is good; his mercy is everlasting; and his truth endureth to all generations."

DRAW
Me NEARER
Today in ...

"I am Thine, O Lord, I have heard Thy voice,
And it told Thy love to me;
But I long to rise in the arms of faith,
And be closer drawn to Thee."

Spiritual Step Count

By Rainy Lehman

I therefore, the prisoner of the Lord, beseech you that ye walk worthy of the vocation wherewith ye are called,

Ephesians 4:1

According to Harvard Health, walking is considered "the closest thing we have to a miracle drug." A few benefits of walking include:

- Improved cardiovascular health
- Increased energy levels
- Improved mood
- Improved memory
- Lowers the risk of dementia
- Boosts immune function

Walking is a great way to improve your overall physical health! While physical health is very important and we should all be better stewards of our "temple" (I Corinthians 6:19), the Bible also tells us in 1 Timothy 4:8a "For bodily exercise profiteth little: but godliness is profitable unto all things ...." Again, not an excuse to neglect our physical health (it may "profit little" but exercise does still profit!), but Paul is teaching Timothy that our spiritual health is far more profitable.

One of the key components to having a healthy spiritual life is to walk with the Lord daily. "But how do we walk with the Lord?," you might ask? Let's consult The Great Physician and see what His Word has to say.

The Bible tells us to:

1. Walk Worthy – Ephesians 4:1, Colossians 1:10, I Thessalonians 2:12
2. Walk Circumspectly – Ephesians 5:15
3. Walk Honestly – Romans 13:13
4. Walk After the Lord – Deuteronomy 13:4
5. Walk in His Statutes – I Kings 8:61, Ezekiel 20:19
6. Walk Uprightly – Proverbs 2:7, Proverbs 14:2
7. Walk in Love – Ephesians 5:2
8. Walk After His Commandments – II John 1:6
9. Walk in the Light – I John 1:7
10. Walk After the Spirit – Romans 8:4, Galatians 5:16
11. Walk by Faith – II Corinthians 5:7
12. Walk in the Old Paths – Jeremiah 6:16
13. Walk not As Gentiles Walk – Ephesians 4:17

There are so many wonderful benefits that come with cultivating a daily walk with the Lord. Want God to strengthen your heart? Walk with Him! Want to have more energy to face the world, the flesh, and the devil? Walk with Him! Want to be in a better mood and have real peace and joy while living in this sin-cursed world? Walk with Him! Need help remembering all that God has done for you and quit forgetting about all that he has blessed you with? Walk with Him! Want to boost your immunity against falling into temptation? Walk with Him!

If nothing else, walk with the Lord daily because, despite our faults and our failures, our holy, precious, Heavenly Father longs to fellowship and walk with us.

DRAW
Me NEARER
Today in ...

"I am Thine, O Lord, I have heard Thy voice,
And it told Thy love to me;
But I long to rise in the arms of faith,
And be closer drawn to Thee."

Don't Follow Your Heart

By Elizabeth Garrett

For ye are bought with a price: therefore glorify God in your body,
and in your spirit, which are God's.

I Corinthians 6:20

You deserve to be happy! You do you! You do what is best for you! You have the right to live your life!

Lately, I have noticed these comments pop up repeatedly as I have scrolled through my Facebook newsfeed. These comments have always been heard in the world ... it is a humanistic, man-centered viewpoint. But these comments are not being written by the world: they are being written by Christians!

To quote James 3:10, "... My brethren, these things ought not so to be."

It is so easy for the world and the world's philosophy to infiltrate our thinking. We must constantly guard against it. Nowhere in Scripture are we told that we deserve happiness or that we are to do what is right for us. It is quite the contrary! Scripture teaches us that all we are and all we have is by the grace and mercy of God! And our duty to our God is to obey Him in all things, not do what is "right" for us. Our life and our decisions are to bring glory to God. "What? know ye not that your body is the temple of the Holy Ghost which is in you, which ye have of God, and ye are not your own? For ye are bought

Our duty to our God is to obey Him in all things, not do what is "right" for us.

with a price: therefore glorify God in your body, and in your spirit, which are God's" (I Corinthians 6:19-20).

Those who are not saved follow the leading of their heart, their flesh. Yet, we as born-again children of God are warned about our hearts. Jeremiah 17:9 says, "The heart is deceitful above all things, and desperately wicked: who can know it?" The days of the Judges in the Bible were perilous times! As we read Judges, we do not have to wonder for long what the problem was. Judges 17:6 says, "In those days there was no king in Israel, but every man did that which was right in his own eyes." When a man chooses to follow the leading of his own heart instead of what God says, the results are disastrous!

As a child of God, I should not base my decisions on what makes me happy or what I consider to be "right" for me.

So, how can we combat this way of thinking?

• **Prepare our hearts**

  Ezra 7:10, "For Ezra had prepared his heart to seek the law of the Lord, and to do it, and to teach in Israel statutes and judgments." The word "prepared" in that verse in the original language means "to establish, to set up, to be firm, to be securely determined." It gives the idea to establish or determine in our hearts. Here Ezra determined in his heart that he would seek God's Word, obey it, and teach it! We must determine in our hearts that we will follow God, no matter what happens or what others do. We should establish the fact that we will not be led by our heart, our emotions, or what "sounds right."

• **Keep our hearts**

  Proverbs 4:23, "Keep thy heart with all diligence; for out of it are the issues of life." The command "to keep" means "to guard (in a good sense), to protect, to watch over." Solomon tells us to guard or protect our hearts with diligence. It is essential that we guard what enters our hearts and what proceeds from our hearts. It requires effort on my part! I cannot simply float through my Christian life with no regard for my heart (my thoughts, emotions, etc). It is a proactive command; I must take the initiative to protect my heart both against what is in my heart and against what would enter my heart from the world.

- **Guide our hearts**

  Proverbs 23:19, "Hear thou, my son, and be wise, and guide thine heart in the way." "Guide" means "to go straight on, to lead on, to set right." As the world shouts its mantra, "Follow your heart!," God commands His child to guide her heart, to lead it, to set it right. Here is where our standard is presented. Paul tells us in Ephesians 4:13, "Till we all come in the unity of the faith, and of the knowledge of the Son of God, unto a perfect man, unto the measure of the stature of the fulness of Christ." Throughout Scripture, we are given instructions on how God wants us to live and how we can be more like Christ. We are to take these commands and guide our hearts in the correct path. We cannot follow the path that our heart chooses; our heart will not choose what pleases God. It will always choose what pleases the flesh.

  May the Lord help us measure our thoughts and words by the standard of His Word and not just repeat phrases that "sound good" to justify wrong decisions or behaviors.

  We do not desire to pattern our thoughts after the philosophy of the lost world around us.

DRAW
Me NEARER
Today in...

"I am Thine, O Lord, I have heard Thy voice,
And it told Thy love to me;
But I long to rise in the arms of faith,
And be closer drawn to Thee."

A Look at Joseph

By Renee Patton

...the Lord was with him....

Genesis 39:23b

For the last few months, Joseph has been at the center of all things at church. I taught about Joseph's life in my Junior Church class, and it seemed every adult Sunday School lesson tied back to Joseph somehow. God has a wonderful way of bringing comfort while in the midst of life's storms. While I continue with so many unknowns of my own, God has given me a few reminders of His goodness, grace, and mercy in Joseph's life and how to continue each day with purpose.

God is in your plans just like He was with Joseph. We must trust God in all we do and do not even see – faith! Trusting God is probably the hardest aspect of faith we must make real in our own lives. Joseph trusted God in the pit, Potiphar's house, and in prison. The tumultuous storm will pass! We must trust in God's goodness and know it will come.

Joseph saw grace and mercy when he interpreted Pharaoh's dreams. Joseph was restored to more than he was before he was put in prison. Joseph's endurance during the challenging times caused him to save his family. The same family who sold him. No one can tell me God does not work in mysterious ways. Imagine being sold, then put as second in command over a country, and eventually saving his family from famine.

God never promises that suffering will cease in this life. Our trust in Him draws us closer to Him. Joseph was pure in his intentions, even after their father died. Joseph took care of his family. No matter the burden or trial, God is there and gives comfort, love, support, and guidance – if only we ask!

Remembering others who have endured like Joseph helps bring peace to our thoughts. Joseph endured like no other; yet was used to save the very family who despised him. Honor God first and foremost. When life is upside down and seemingly falling apart – honor God. Remember Joseph and how he was blessed after such turmoil. Joseph had to keep his heart right and so must we! God was with Joseph and He will be with each of us also!

DRAW *Me* NEARER

Today in...

"I am Thine, O Lord, I have heard Thy voice,
And it told Thy love to me;
But I long to rise in the arms of faith,
And be closer drawn to Thee."

About The Authors

Each author has been handpicked because of their Christian testimony. God has gifted each writer with incredibly versatile perspectives of the Christian life. These godly ladies come from all walks of life including pastor's wives and daughters, missionary wives, church staff ladies, and faithful church members. Their written words of wisdom are sure to bless your heart.

To know more about our writers please visit:
thehighlyfavouredlife.com/our-story

Salvation Made Simple

By Renee Patton

Admit. One must first admit they are a sinner. Romans 3:10 states, "As it is written, There is none righteous, no, not one." Sin is everywhere and we all commit sin, many times without even trying. Perhaps in a conversation, we say something innocently, then realize it was not correct. That, my friend, is lying. Of course, murder is a sin that is seen and felt by those affected. However, lying is too. Jeremiah reminds one that "The heart is deceitful above all things, and desperately wicked: who can know it?" (17:9). A baby does not have to be told how to sin, it is simply in our nature. One must admit they are a sinner otherwise we make God a liar as found in I John 1:10, "If we say that we have not sinned, we make him a liar, and his word is not in us."

Believe. One must believe Jesus came to this earth to be born and die for our sins. "For God so loved the world, that he gave his only begotten Son, that whosoever believeth in him should not peish, but have everlasting life" (John 3:16). God desires that we should not perish, thus the choice is ours. God gives man the opportunity for salvation if man would take it. Romans 5:8 states "But God commendeth his love toward us, in that, while we were yet sinners,

Christ died for us." Webster's 1828 Dictionary defines commendeth as entrusts or gives. So, God gave us His love through His Son, Jesus. Furthermore, Romans 5:19 shows how sin came from Adam and is made righteous through Christ, "For as by one man's disobedience [Adam] many were made sinners [mankind], so by the obedience of one [Jesus] shall many [mankind] be made righteous."

Confess. Confession is made with one's own mouth. The words must come from the person alone. Romans 10:9 talks of both confession and believing, "That if thou shalt confess with thy mouth the lord Jesus, and shalt believe in thine heart that God hath raised him from the dead, thou shalt be saved." The key is I have to confess to God. My husband or friend cannot confess for me. While God gives man the opportunity on earth, there will be a time every knee will bow and confess God is Lord, "For it is written, As I live, saith the Lord, every knee shall bow to me, and every tongue shall confess to God" (Romans 14:11).

To see more resources on salvation visit:

https://www.thehighlyfavouredlife.com/simple-salvation

If you made this decision, please contact us at *highlyfavouredlife @gmail.com.*

We would love to rejoice with you in the new life you now have in Christ.

Made in the USA
Columbia, SC
06 May 2025

57515704R00098